PART OF THE LIFE SCULPTOR BLUEPRINT SERIES

HOW TO TALK TO ANYONE

SOCIAL SKILLS MADE EASY

PROVEN STRATEGIES FOR
Mastering Small Talk, Confident Speaking,
Approachable Communication,
and Networking Success

AF392575

Written By:

JACK WOLF

POSG

https://POSG.life

Contents

GET THIS BOOK - FREE
Your Personal Power Move Starts Now

TIRED OF BEING WALKED ON, TALKED OVER, OR PUSHED PAST YOUR LIMITS?

This guide is your no-BS playbook for dealing with chronic boundary crashers—without guilt, self-doubt, or second-guessing. You'll get the exact steps to stand firm, speak up, and stop bending to please.

HERE'S THE KICKER: THIS BOOK IS 100% FREE.
No strings. Just tools that work.

SCAN THE CODE OR VISIT THE LINK BELOW
TO CLAIM YOUR INSTANT DOWNLOAD
AND GET ON THE LIST FOR FUTURE
EXCLUSIVE RELEASES—BEFORE ANYONE ELSE

posg.life/RespectBoundaries

SUPER-CHARGE YOUR CONFIDENCE
With the Companion Guided Journal

As you dive into *How to Talk to Anyone*, you'll see what's possible when connection clicks. But reading is one thing. Living it? Whole different story. That's where this journal steps in.

The Daily Confidence Building Exercises Guided Journal is your day-by-day training ground to sharpen your communication skills, crush social anxiety, and grow confidence that doesn't flinch—no matter the room, the pressure, or the stakes.

Are you tired of feeling unsure in conversations? Second-guessing yourself in meetings? Freezing up in social situations and walking away thinking, "Why didn't I say that?"

This journal is your answer. It's practical. It's powerful. And it's built for action.

Each daily exercise is short, sharp, and built to:

- Build your self-image

- Boost your assertiveness

- Improve your body language

- Supercharge your conversation skills

- Rewire how you talk to yourself—and the world

Whether you're prepping for an interview, building deeper relationships, or just ready to stop playing small in your social life, this journal gets you there.

Confidence isn't luck. It's practice. This journal gives you the tools—and the plan—to make it real.

DAILY CONFIDENCE BUILDING EXERCISES
Guided Journal to Sharpen Your Voice, Build Boldness, and Master Everyday Conversations

BY: JACK WOLF

Available for Purchase:
https://posg.life/BuyDailyConfidence

Introduction

Desperate for Breakthough

Of all the dumb luck in the world, I got robbed at birth.

I came into this world sharp and capable, but without the one thing I needed to thrive: social confidence.

I had thoughts, insights, things to say… but the moment I opened my mouth, my body betrayed me. Sweaty armpits. Scattered thoughts. Face flushed. Heart racing like I was being hunted. Every conversation felt like a high-stakes ambush. And eye contact? Forget it—I'd rather skydive without a chute.

Sound familiar?

If even a part of that hits, good. You're in the right place.

Because I broke out. I turned it around. I went from dodging small talk to leading boardroom negotiations. From panic attacks over "hello" to becoming a confident, clear communicator. From hiding in the background to holding my space with purpose.

And now? I teach people how to do the same.

But I wasn't always this guy.

I used to be the one stuck in his own head. A young man, drowning in self-doubt and social anxiety. On the outside, just another quiet guy. Inside? Starving—for ease, for connection, for confidence.

I wanted to be free from awkwardness. But I was raised in an environment wired for fear. I didn't grow up with occasional anxiety. It was the air I breathed. So I stayed small. I avoided discomfort as if it were fire.

Until one day, I'd had enough.

I didn't wish for change. I worked for it. It took years of trial and error—facing fears, taking hits, and learning the hard way what works and what's absolute garbage when it comes to overcoming social anxiety.

Slowly, things shifted. I stopped bailing on conversations. I quit dodging invites. Eventually, I made a bold move. I started opening up with my coworkers. Not once. Not twice. Often. That one decision sparked a ripple I never saw coming.

One habit became momentum. Momentum built relationships. Relationships grew confidence. Confidence fueled bigger moves.

Next thing I knew, I wasn't just surviving social situations—I was thriving in them. I was forming deeper connections. I was dating. I was opening myself to a life I used to think was for other people.

Was it easy? No.

Was it worth it? More than I ever imagined.

I'm not special. I'm just done letting fear make my choices.

And now, I have a new purpose: leading others to the same waters I drank from.

I can't force you to drink. But I can take you there. I can give you the tools, the mindset shifts, the exact steps that pulled me—and so many others—out of social anxiety's grip. You just have to be willing to trust the process. Some things you won't believe until you see them working in your own life.

No fluff. No shortcuts. Just battle-tested tools that actually work to rewire how you connect with others.

So let me ask you—do you feel yourself holding back in conversations? Do you hesitate to speak up because you're afraid of rejection? Do social situations drain the life out of you because you're too caught up in your own head?

Even if social anxiety isn't your battle, maybe you're struggling with communication itself. Maybe you don't know how to strike up conversations, how to carry them, how to connect in a way that feels natural.

If any of that sounds like you, then this book is your battle plan.

You're going to learn how to flip the script on social anxiety, rewire your confidence, and let go of the fear gripping your every move. Here's what's coming:

Part I: Start With You

This is where it all begins—not with tips, but with truth. The first three chapters help you stop hiding and start owning who you are. You'll build real confidence from the inside out. No more fear running your interactions. No more shrinking. It's time to feel solid in your own skin and walk into any room like you belong there.

Part II: Power Tools to Talk to Anyone

Now we get tactical. These chapters load your belt with tools that cut through small talk and spark real connections fast. You'll master the rhythm of great conversation and learn to listen so sharply it disarms people. This is how you go from awkward to unforgettable.

Part III: Speak Bold. Live Bigger.

Here's where you level up from competent to magnetic. You'll learn to lead with empathy, hold the line with boundaries, and build trust that actually lasts. Whether it's your relationships, your career, or your confidence—we're done playing small. You're here to speak boldly and live bigger.

Just like me.

This book isn't about theory. It's about results. It's about showing up in your own life instead of sitting on the sidelines, wondering what it would be like to feel socially fearless.

By the end of this, you'll be holding your own in conversations with anyone, anywhere.

No more awkward. No more hesitating. No more feeling like a prisoner in your own mind. It's time to step up, take action, and own your social confidence.

One Last Thing: Take Action

This book isn't for passive reading. It's for doing. Every challenge is a shot at freedom—your escape plan. Don't just think. Don't just read. Do.

Fear gains power whenever we allow it to stop us from moving toward freedom. The only way to beat it is to act despite it.

So, make a promise to yourself right now.

Enough waiting. Enough overthinking. Life won't wait. It's your turn now. So stand up, speak up, and go get it.

You'll see action steps throughout this book for a reason.
They're not homework. They're launch pads—built to ignite something specific in you: hope, clarity, courage. Maybe even expose a lie that's been running the show behind the scenes.

You don't *have* to do them.
No one's grading you.

But if you want change that sticks, you've got to move.
Fear feeds on hesitation. It thrives in the shadows of "maybe later." But the second you act—even with shaking hands and a shaky voice—that's when fear starts packing its bags.

So here's the ask:
From this page forward, stop waiting to feel ready.

Take the step. Break the cycle. Choose freedom over familiarity.

You want out of the cage?
Rattle the door and walk through.

Part I

Start With You

Chapters 1 – 3

"The truly scary thing about undiscovered lies is that they have a greater capacity to diminish us than exposed ones. They erode our strength, our self-esteem, our very foundation."

—Cheryl Hughes

How to Talk to Anyone doesn't start with charm; it starts with the most important conversation of all—the one you have with yourself. Part I is about ownership. Not posing or polishing, but real, unshakable ownership of your identity, your fear, and your voice.

This isn't about memorizing clever lines or improving your small talk. Want real connection? Presence that hits like thunder? This is where you own who you are and learn to carry it like a force.

Don't wait to feel ready. Fear doesn't fade with time. Confidence doesn't come with age. It's earned. It's claimed. Get ready. First, we tear down. Then we build something real.

There's dynamite in you, my friend. Let's light the fuse.

Chapter 1

Step Into Your Real Power

"You're unlovable. A fraud. A joke. Show them the real you, and they'll run."

For years, that voice lived inside me—low, relentless, and cruel. It whispered at first. Then it laughed. Then it roared. No matter what I achieved, it followed, convincing me that survival meant hiding behind a mask.

And for a long time, I did.

I built a version of myself that was safer. More likable. More forgettable.

I couldn't change who I was, but I was dead set on making sure no one else ever saw it.

Ever put on a mask just to get through the day? At work? Around friends? Family gatherings?

Maybe, like I did, you still do it. Because being truly seen? That's terrifying.

What if they judge you? What if they don't accept you? Worse—what if they confirm your worst fear: that you're not enough?

If you've ever felt that, you're not broken—and you're not alone.

I used to sit in a group, mind racing. I had something to say. Something real. Something good.

But as I opened my mouth, the voice would strike: "What if you sound stupid?"

I laughed along instead. Said nothing. Disappeared again.

Everybody wrestles with how much of themselves they dare to show the world. Some people own it—bold, unfiltered, unapologetic. Others shrink, waiting for permission that never comes.

Here's the truth: you don't need permission.

You already have the right to be seen. To be heard. To be fully, unapologetically YOU.

And if that makes some people uncomfortable? Screw it. That's their problem, not yours.

I know what you're thinking: "That's easy for you to say. I've tried before. The anxiety is too powerful." And you're right. There is no cure for the physical effects of fear. And it's not about flipping a magical switch.

It's about flipping a mindset.

But once you understand the power of the right perspective? Everything shifts.

Awkwardness fades. Conversations flow. Confidence stops feeling like an act and starts feeling like your natural state.

This chapter is your roadmap to get there.

Think this is just feel-good talk? Let me prove it.

One of My First Breakthroughs

Rewind the clock to when I couldn't string two words together without sweating through my shirt.

I wasn't just awkward—I was anxious, shut down, and convinced that everyone could see how out of place I felt. My brain would blank out like a power failure, and my body? Full-on panic mode. We're talking fight-or-flight chaos... just from saying "hello."

So, how'd I begin to discover the right mindset? How did I go from shutdown mode to actually feeling at home with other people?

I'd love to tell you it was some genius plan.

It wasn't.

It was a happy accident.

One of my first real jobs was as an IT specialist. Young guy. New to the game. I provided technical support for a department of 300 people. And to be honest? I wanted to hide in the back office with the other techs and wait for people to call for help. It felt safer there. No small talk. No awkward moments. Just screens and silence.

But I wasn't hired to hide. I was hired to help. Comfort wouldn't help me grow. So I made a choice.

Instead of waiting for trouble tickets, I started walking the floor. Up and down the aisles. Making myself visible. If someone's system crashed or their printer flipped out, I was already there—fixing it before they could even hit the panic button.

And little by little, something started to shift.

At first, people just nodded. A quick "thanks" here or there. But the more I showed up—the more I kept walking that floor, fixing problems before they became disasters—the more the energy changed.

What I didn't expect? People loved knowing I was there. Even when they didn't need help.

People started smiling when they saw me coming. Cracking jokes. Calling out, "There he is—my guy!" They didn't just appreciate the help. They welcomed me in. Like I belonged there.

Not because I forced it. But because I kept showing up.

That's when I realized I wasn't just solving tech problems. I was building trust. One walk, one fix, one conversation at a time.

I leaned into it. I started making small talk while troubleshooting. I'd ask how their weekend went or check in on the cat they mentioned last time. I wasn't trying to perform—I was just learning how to be me in public.

Somewhere in that rhythm, I accepted something I'd never believed before:

My presence had value.

All my life, I believed I was a burden. I was invisible. I was too weird, too awkward, or too much. I was unfortunately me.

But people didn't confirm those fears—so I was now forced to question them.

The anxiety didn't disappear overnight. In fact, it hasn't completely gone away to this day. And every day was a recurring fight to dive into those freezing waters of connection.

But over time, I adjusted to the cold. I adapted. I built muscle. I learned to belong.

What changed?

I did.

Not because I was special. Not because I had all the answers or found the right supplements to calm the raging storm of anxiety.

But because I kept showing up anyway.

If I can do that?

So can you.

This isn't about becoming someone new. This is about reclaiming who you've always been underneath the fear, the doubt, and the endless cycle of wondering what other people think. It's time to stop hiding. It's time to stop filtering yourself.

Because the world doesn't need another carefully curated, socially acceptable version of you.

It needs you.

> "Your time is limited, so don't waste it living someone else's life."
>
> Steve Jobs

The Importance of Self-Acceptance

Here's a life-altering truth: if you don't accept yourself, you're setting yourself up for a lifetime of playing small. And playing small is a tragedy because the world doesn't need a muted, watered-down version of you. It needs the real you, full force, no holding back.

But before we dive into how to get there, let's define what self-acceptance actually means.

Self-acceptance is owning every flaw, strength, and quirk without apology—and without waiting for a permission slip. Study after study backs it up: the people who own themselves—without conditions—build stronger lives, stronger relationships, stronger everything. (*"The Path to Unconditional Self-Acceptance,"* n.d.).

And that part's important. Because self-acceptance doesn't mean stagnation. It doesn't mean settling. It means being radically honest with yourself so that you have a foundation strong enough to grow from. If you want to be authentic with other people, you have to first be authentic with yourself. That's where confidence comes from. That's where true social ease builds.

People who own who they are have a different energy. They walk into a room without second-guessing their presence. They acknowledge their weaknesses without self-pity and own their strengths without arrogance. They don't need a hundred people nodding in approval to feel solid in their skin. And if that sounds impossible to you right now, I want you to stick with me because you're about to see just how much this can transform your life.

Let's break this down into some real-life scenarios. Because self-acceptance isn't just a *nice idea.* It affects everything, from your career to your relationships to how you handle stress.

Picture this: Your boss dumps a high-stakes project on your lap—tight deadlines, moving parts everywhere—and doubt punches you square in the chest.

Or you're standing in front of an important client, about to speak, and your palms are slick with fear.

Doubt doesn't just show up when you chase something big. It slams you when you try to step out of your comfort zone at all.

But here's the difference:

If you don't accept yourself, you freeze. You shrink. You make excuses and you prove to yourself that your own self-doubt is right.

If you do accept yourself? You move anyway. You see the gaps in your skillset, sure—but you don't let them chain you down. You own them. You grow through them. You walk into the room carrying the work you've done, not the fear of how you'll look.

So ask yourself: philosophically, who are you going to be? The one who gets in your own way? Or the one who will learn to acknowledge your weaknesses without letting them dictate your actions?

Because when you **refuse** to accept yourself—when you **fight against** who you are, when you live in constant self-doubt—you don't just struggle socially.

You struggle, period.

And if you do that long enough, it starts to take a toll. Anxiety, depression, destructive habits. These things don't come out of nowhere. They come from living in a state of constant resistance against yourself.

Self-acceptance isn't about feeling good.

It's about breaking the cycle so you can finally live.

How to Practice Self-Acceptance

How do you shift from self-doubt to self-acceptance? It's not just a quick decision—it's consistently training yourself to see and treat yourself differently.

Think of this like a golf course. You won't win the game with just one skill. You need the full range—power off the tee, finesse on the green, steady aim in the final putt, and everything in between.

Some folks can drive a ball halfway to the moon but choke when it's time to sink it with a final tap.

The same goes here.

You might crush it in one area of connection but fall flat in another. That's normal. That's human.

So, as you read the following sections, spot the gaps. Be honest. What's strong? What's struggling? Those weak spots? That's where you'll aim your energy. That's where the real growth lives.

Let's start where all lasting change begins—your values.

First, embrace your values. Your values make up the foundation of who you are. They shape your decisions, your priorities, and the way you see the world. If you don't accept your own values, you'll find yourself bending to fit other people's worldviews—which leaves you wondering if you even belong anywhere. Know what matters to you, and don't compromise it just to be more palatable to others.

Second, forgive yourself for past mistakes. Look, beating yourself up over things you *could've* done differently is a waste of energy. It keeps you in a loop that serves no purpose. The past is done. You can't go back and edit it, but you can move forward with wisdom instead of regret. Stop punishing yourself for being human.

Stop apologizing for things that aren't yours. You know what I'm talking about—the automatic "sorry" that flies out before you even realize it. Here's the truth: not everything is on you. The weight of the world is not yours to carry. The sooner you internalize that, the lighter you'll feel.

Avoid the comparison trap. Everyone is running their own race. If you spend your life measuring your progress against someone else's highlight reel, you'll always feel like you're behind. Instead of looking at what they have, ask yourself what *you* actually want—and why. When you stop chasing someone else's version of success, you free yourself up to actually build a life that makes sense for you.

Big one: stop handing your life over to other people's opinions. Your mind will insist that you must impress them. Don't listen. It will tell you that you need approval, that you need to be liked, that you need to fit a mold to be accepted. You have to ignore that inner voice. You are the one in charge of your own life. No one else. The second you take back control, everything changes.

Call out your inner drama. Watch your patterns, your thoughts, your triggers. Notice how much energy you waste on worry. The more you see your own behaviors, the easier they are to change.

And above all, make self-acceptance a habit, not just a belief. It's not something you wake up with one day and never have to work on again. It's a practice. But the more you commit to it, the easier it gets. And one day, without even realizing it, you'll look back and wonder how you ever lived any other way.

Allow me to offer a shameless plug because I so firmly believe in its power to help those struggling. If you're truly ready to start rewiring the mindsets that have been keeping you stuck, check out my book:

Fix Your Habits, Transform Your Life:
Proven Strategies To Break Bad Habits And Create Lasting Change Without Endless Frustration

It isn't just another "feel-good" guide—it's a **blueprint** for strategically using your habits at the biological level to build unshakable confidence, embrace the needed mindset, and start becoming the person you're meant to be.

Get all the details here: https://posg.life/habits.

Whatever you do, commit to this journey wholeheartedly. Every second you doubt yourself is a second stolen from the life you're meant to own.

Teeing Off: Authenticity

When you stop caring what others think, that's when you're truly free. But let's get one thing straight—self-acceptance doesn't mean throwing common sense out the window.

You still need to function in the world. You don't show up to your corporate job in a swimsuit, and you don't belt out raunchy drinking songs at your grandma's funeral—unless, of course, she specifically requested it in her final moments. Then, by all means, honor that legend.

So, what exactly *is* authenticity? Let's take a look at it from a psychological standpoint:

Authentic people don't fake it. They align their actions with their values—and they live like they mean it (*Authenticity* | "*Psychology Today United Kingdom*," n.d.).

Read that again.

It isn't only about preference. It's ultimately about values.

Real authenticity starts with the self-awareness to reflect your personal values without hesitation and own a strong sense of identity in your relationships. Sound familiar? That's because this ties directly into what we discussed about self-acceptance.

When you accept yourself, you naturally start living authentically.

And let me tell you, there is no better feeling in the world than dropping the mask you've been wearing and stepping into life as the real you. It's like shedding a heavy weight you didn't even realize you were carrying. Suddenly, you're not filtering every word anymore—you're just being. And life finally feels so much lighter.

And the best part? When you live authentically, your ability to handle emotions and navigate social situations skyrockets. You stop wasting emotional bandwidth on fear and overthinking. You stop twisting yourself into knots, wondering how people will react. Instead, you remain aligned to what matters without question.

There's no need to waste energy checking in with yourself. Instead, direct that energy toward **owning your happiness.**

Once you stop second-guessing yourself, you stop being socially awkward. You start realizing that the things you once saw as weird or different about yourself? They're your superpowers. And when you lean into them, you tap into a level of confidence and personal power that most people only dream about. Beyond that, you earn peace and quiet in your soul.

Written by someone so socially awkward that he never made a real impact until he dared to show the world who he really was. Weakness and all.

How to Get Comfortable with Your Uniqueness

The first step to celebrating your uniqueness? Get to know yourself.

Yeah, I know—it sounds so obvious. If you'd stop rolling your eyes, you'd be shocked by how many people have no idea what lights them up. They've spent so long trying to belong that they forgot who they are.

I've had friends who actually didn't know what they valued. They just borrowed whatever the herd believed and called it their own. Don't be that person.

Own your perspective. Don't rent it.

Start paying attention. What excites you? What drains you? What values would you never compromise on? If you don't know, figure it out. Journaling helps. Meditation helps. Even a simple personality test can snap on the lights. The goal is simple: **own who you are, fully and unapologetically.**

Inventory your passions. Quick gut check: If you could start a 30-minute conversation right now with zero prep, what would you want to talk about? Whatever pops in your mind first, that's a window into what fires you up.

Embrace your quirks. They make life interesting. They're not flaws; they're fingerprints. Dip your French fries in ice cream? Own it. Only work to movie soundtracks? Perfect. Always wear mismatched socks because it feels lucky? Heck yes. People don't bond with *perfect*. They bond with *real*.

Don't just sit back in your comfort zone—kick it over. Apply for the dream job. Jump out of the plane. Take the dance class even if you've got two left feet. Take yourself out to dinner and own that solo table.

Life's not meant to be watched from the sidelines. Stop avoiding pain. Get in the game. Gradually, if necessary. But go.

And when you step into the world? Wear what makes you feel powerful. Clothes aren't fabric; they're armor. If it fires you up, wear it. If it drags you down, ditch it.

That outer armor matters—but the real power move? How you treat people. Confidence isn't just about how you look. It's about the impact you make on the people around you.

The Power of Kindness and Perspective

People won't be attracted by how authentic you are if you are an authentic jerk.

Be kind.

You don't have to be the center of attention to make an impact. You just have to be someone who adds value.

Real confidence isn't loud. It's steady. It's quiet strength that hits harder than volume.

Not the fake 'look at me' kind. The real kind—the kind you do when no one's clapping. Treat people the way you'd want to be treated, even when they don't deserve it. Because at the end of the day, you never know what someone else is going through. A simple act of kindness might turn their entire day around.

Owning Your Strengths, Acknowledging Your Weaknesses

You've got talents—everyone does. Maybe you're artistic. Maybe you're a beast in the gym. Maybe you're the person everyone comes to for advice. Whatever it is, own it. Don't downplay it. Don't brush it off.

At the same time, don't be afraid to acknowledge where you're *not* strong. That's not failure—it's awareness. Knowing where you need to improve gives you the power to actually get better. Have self-awareness without beating yourself up; get comfortable with your own blueprint.

As you grow, take time to reflect. Connect the dots between your past experiences, your choices, and your values. The more you understand your own patterns, the more control you have over your future.

This helps you embrace discomfort.

And stop comparing yourself to others. Comparison is a game rigged to make you lose. There will always be someone with more money, a better job, a fancier house. So what? Their path isn't your path. Their story isn't your story. The only person you should be measuring yourself against is who you were yesterday.

The Bottom Line

Living authentically isn't about getting permission from the world. It's about giving yourself permission to be exactly who you are. No filtering, no shrinking, no apologies.

Once you get there, you won't just walk into a room; you'll own it. You won't just be another face in the crowd—you'll be **you**, boldly and unapologetically. And that? That's a game-changer.

Own it boldly. Adapt when you must. But never forget who you are.

Time for Some Action!

Embrace Your Quirks: Choose one personal quirk and celebrate it in a conversation or on social media.

Authentic Self vs. Adaptive Self

Let's talk about balance.

Even when you're fully embracing your authentic self, there are going to be moments when your adaptive self steps in. And guess what? That's not always a bad thing. Your adaptive self is the version of you that adjusts—sometimes for survival, sometimes for strategy, and sometimes just because wearing a suit instead of beach shorts keeps you employed.

Not every situation calls for full-throttle authenticity. If you're in a dangerous situation where speaking your truth could put you at risk—physically, emotionally, or otherwise—then put the mask on until you're safe. Self-preservation comes first. But being adaptive for safety is one thing—being adaptive because you're scared of being judged is another. That's where a lot of people get stuck.

These are your guide rails.

You don't want to overcorrect and become so adaptive that you slip right back into people-pleasing mode, completely losing touch with your authentic self. You spent too much time breaking free from that to end up back where you started. Authenticity takes practice. It takes deliberate choices. And part of that is knowing when to be fully, unapologetically YOU—and when to adapt without losing yourself in the process.

The key? Discernment. Become aware of when you're choosing to adapt for *good* reasons—like showing respect in a setting where full-blown honesty might not be appropriate. (Because, yeah, telling the truth doesn't mean you have to be insulting.) There's a difference between being honest and being reckless with your words. Stay true to your values. Make decisions that align with who you are. Keep pushing toward self-improvement.

And being authentic doesn't mean staying the same forever. You can be *you* and still grow. In fact, that's the only way real growth happens.

Knowing who you are is one thing. Carrying it into real life? That's the next battle.

Using Individuality to Aid You in Social Situations

You can own yourself all you want, but you still have to navigate a world that's bigger than you. Family, friendships, work environments, social circles, communities, and cultures. And whether you like it or not, navigating those spaces requires some level of social awareness. That doesn't mean abandoning who you are; it means figuring out how to stay authentically YOU while still functioning in a world that's full of people who may think, act, and believe differently.

Sometimes, the culture you grew up in doesn't match the world you step into as an adult. Maybe you were raised in a strict religious environment but later found your beliefs shifting. Maybe you grew up in a small, insulated community and now find yourself in a wildly diverse city where people's worldviews are drastically different from yours. That kind of transition can be jarring—but here's the cool part: the more you embrace your authentic self, the easier it becomes to find where you fit.

Self-identity and group identity don't have to be at odds. You can belong to a community without losing yourself in it. Think about a sports team—when they're on the field, they're all working toward a common goal. They share an identity as athletes, teammates, and competitors. But when they step off the field, they're still individuals. Some love to cook, some are obsessed with sci-fi, some play guitar, some are deeply into video games. The group identity doesn't erase who they are—it just adds another layer to it.

This applies to every social dynamic. You don't have to conform to everything, but you do need to find a balance between being uniquely yourself and integrating into the world around you. The need to belong is wired into us as humans, but you can fulfill that need without sacrificing your individuality.

That being said, there will be times when a group—or even a family—makes you feel like being yourself isn't enough. If you ever feel like the expectations of the people around you are forcing you to shrink, mask, or betray who you are, that's a problem.

That's your signal. Step back. Ask yourself: *Is this really where I want to be? Can I still love them without being pulled into conflict?*

Because if belonging costs you your soul, it's not belonging—it's surrender. And the people who love you should never demand surrender.

Thriving in a Group Without Losing Yourself

Let's assume you've found your place among your people.

When you're part of a team, a family, a social circle, or a work environment, it's easy to slip into comparison mode. You start measuring your success, happiness, or worth based on what everyone else around you is doing. Someone else gets the promotion, the engagement ring, the dream vacation, and suddenly, your own accomplishments feel *less than*. Stop that.

The second you start comparing your life to someone else's, you're setting yourself up to lose. No one else has your story. No one else has walked your exact path. Trying to measure your life against someone else's is like judging a fish on how well it can fly. It's nonsense and discouraging.

Instead of comparison, choose celebration. Be genuinely happy when someone else wins. Congratulate them. Cheer them on. Why? Because their success doesn't take anything away from you. Your time will come—but not if you waste all your energy resenting someone else's success instead of working toward your own.

All of this—how you carry yourself, how you treat others, how you respond when life puts someone else in the spotlight—all leads to one thing: owning who you are without apology.

Moving Forward with Self-Acceptance and Confidence

We've covered a lot in this chapter. We've talked about what it means to accept yourself, to own your uniqueness, to find balance between being authentic and being adaptive, and to thrive in social situations without losing yourself in the crowd.

But now, it's time to go even deeper. Because even when you're fully embracing who you are, there's one more major hurdle to tackle—social anxiety.

And that's what we're taking on next. That's right. We're not going to skim over that elephant in the room.

If you've ever felt the crushing weight of social anxiety—if you've ever overanalyzed every word after a conversation, avoided eye contact, felt frozen in social settings, or convinced yourself that you're just "bad at talking to people"—this next chapter is for you. We're not just going to talk about what social anxiety *is;* we're going to cut its legs off.

You've already taken the first step by embracing who you are. Now, it's time to finish what you started. Smile; there's no turning back now.

This is where your old fears go to die.

Let's do this.

***

Ending With a Bang!

Enough waiting. Enough hesitating. If you want to see real change, you need to **take massive action right now**. This is about momentum. The faster you move, the quicker you break free.

1. **Journal for Self-Discovery**: Writing isn't just about dumping thoughts onto paper—it's about discovering what's really going on in your head. It helps you track patterns, call out your excuses, and get brutally honest with yourself. If you need a head start, grab the free ***How to Talk to Anyone Guided Journal*** at https://posg.life/FreeDCBE. If you're the kind of person who likes something physical in your hands, there's a paperback copy waiting for you on Amazon at https://posg.life/buyJournal. The sooner you start, the sooner you break through.

2. **Challenge Your Fear:** Identify a fear that holds you back and take a small step to confront it. This will encourage you to declare war on anxiety, reminding you that it does not have a hold on you.

3. **Seek Feedback**: Ask a trusted friend or family member for honest feedback on how you present yourself authentically. Ponder their feedback and record ways you might adjust to become more authentic.

4. **Stop Caring About Others' Opinions**: Your challenge: In the next 24 hours, do something you've been afraid to do because of what others might think. No waiting. No overthinking. The longer you hesitate, the stronger the fear gets. So pick something—right now—and commit. What will it be?

Chapter 1 Recap: Step Into Your Real Power

- **You don't need permission to be real.** You already have the right.

- **Masks feel deceptively safe.** Living masked kills your soul.

- **Self-acceptance isn't a feeling.** It's a weapon you choose every day.

- **Authenticity isn't reckless.** It's unstoppable when rooted in truth.

- **You don't fit in by shrinking.** You own your space by expanding.

Takeaway:

You're not here to shrink. Start living wide open and unapologetic—because the world doesn't change by people who blend in. It is changed by people who dare to press into building relationships.

Chapter 2

No More Hiding

You step into the room, and it slams into you like a wall. The air thickens. Your chest tightens. Your pulse pounds in your eye sockets like a war drum. Every nerve in your body is screaming: **Get out fast.**

But you can't.

You're frozen.

Standing there, every nerve on fire, convinced that every single person in the room is staring, judging, picking apart every awkward move you make.

Your mind starts its usual ambush. What if I say something stupid? What if I freeze? What if they see right through me—see how awkward, uncomfortable, and out of place I really am?

You're trapped in your own head, and the only thing louder than the noise in your brain is the overwhelming need to escape.

Sound familiar? If it does, you're not alone. But more importantly, you're not stuck.

Social anxiety is a beast, and if you've ever felt its grip, you know how brutal it can be. It doesn't just make you nervous. It makes you feel like a prisoner in your own mind, convinced that the only way to avoid disaster is to disappear. But here's the truth: avoiding social situations doesn't make the anxiety go away. It feeds it. And every time you let fear win, it grows stronger.

That ends now.

This chapter is about taking that fear, putting it in a chokehold, and taking your power back. It's time to stop overanalyzing every interaction, stop letting anxiety call the shots, and start becoming the person you know you're capable of being.

You don't need to be perfect. You don't need to impress anyone. You just need to start.

For example, take Tobias Atkins, life-transformation coach and best-selling author. He spent years believing he was just born shy, that confidence was something other people had, and that social anxiety was just part of who he was. He figured he'd always be the guy who faded into the background, the one who stayed quiet even when he had something to say. He didn't realize that social anxiety was more than just personality—it was something he could challenge and change.

Tobias didn't grow up in an environment that encouraged open conversations about emotions. He never learned how to express himself, and the more he struggled, the more isolated he felt. He wanted to connect with people, to feel at ease in his own skin, but instead, he felt trapped—awkward, uncomfortable, and constantly second-guessing himself. His self-doubt spiraled into depression because, deep down, he wanted to engage with the world. He just didn't know how.

At 27, Tobias Atkins hit rock bottom. Hard. Social anxiety wasn't just a struggle. It was a prison. He was convinced this was it—he'd always be stuck on the sidelines, too afraid to speak up, too trapped in his own head to live.

Rock bottom wasn't some dramatic event—it was the slow, crushing weight of self-loathing, the belief that he was just wired wrong and there was nothing he could do about it.

But something inside him refused to settle. Instead of accepting his fate, he made a bold move—he went all in on his own recovery, throwing down over $35,000 on alternative therapies, testing, failing, and pushing himself through every uncomfortable challenge.

He made progress. Most importantly, he began to believe he wasn't powerless.

It wasn't easy. It wasn't instant. But through sheer determination, he built his way out, challenging every negative thought that had kept him small, learning to accept himself instead of tearing himself down, and forcing himself into social situations until the fear lost its grip. He didn't just survive social anxiety. He conquered it.

And today? He's not just managing his anxiety—he's helping others do the same.

That's what's possible. That's what's waiting for you. Social anxiety isn't an incurable life sentence. It's a challenge. And challenges? They're meant to be overcome.

It may go away completely for you. It may not. But it doesn't have the right to own you. You can learn to take back your power.

So, are you ready to stop letting fear run your life? Let's press forward.

Understanding Social Anxiety

Let's call it what it is. Social anxiety isn't just "being shy." It's not just getting a little nervous before a speech or feeling awkward at a party. It's a full-blown, relentless attack that makes even everyday interactions feel like a battlefield.

Social Anxiety Disorder (SAD) isn't some minor inconvenience; it's a mental health condition that can grip your life in a chokehold, making it nearly impossible to enjoy the world around you. And if you're dealing with it, you know exactly what I mean.

Understanding social anxiety isn't about labeling yourself—it's about knowing what you're up against so you can fight back.

If you are like I was, your heart starts pounding the second you step into a crowded room. Your face turns red, your palms sweat, and suddenly, your own voice feels like it's locked away somewhere you can't reach. Your brain either goes blank or speeds up so fast you can't keep up with your own thoughts. The second you open your mouth, you're convinced you sound stupid. Every laugh, every glance in your direction feels like confirmation that you're being judged, mocked, or silently rejected.

And so, you start avoiding situations that trigger it.

You dodge eye contact.

Shrink into the background.

Skip out on social gatherings.

Stay in your comfort zone, where at least the anxiety can't reach you.

But here's the brutal truth: every time you avoid a social situation out of fear, you're reinforcing the belief that you can't handle it.

And that belief is a lie.

Now, let's get one thing straight—social anxiety isn't just "in your head." Your brain has been wired for fear. And guess what? That wiring can be rewired. There's actual science behind it. More on that in this book.

Here's more great news! To date, no one's found a meaningful "social anxiety gene." Even if they did, biology isn't a life sentence. There is always room for adaptation.

Here is some bad news. If your brain's fear response is cranked up too high, social situations can start feeling like actual threats, even when there's no real danger. And let's not forget life experience. If you've been bullied, criticized, or made to feel like you don't belong, your brain wires itself to expect rejection.

Some people grow up in environments that fuel anxiety—maybe they had overly strict, critical, or overprotective parents who made them feel like public mistakes were unforgivable. So, anxiety has just become a part of everyday life.

But let's be real. None of that changes the fact that social anxiety can wreck your life if you let it. It's not just about feeling nervous in crowds. It's about the opportunities you don't take because you're afraid of embarrassing yourself. It's about the jobs you don't go for because the thought of an interview makes you want to throw up. It's about the friendships and relationships you miss out on because your anxiety convinces you people won't accept you. Left unchecked, it can spiral into isolation, addiction, depression—even thoughts of giving up altogether.

If any of this sounds familiar, listen up: social anxiety will not become your destiny. It's your enemy—one that can be tackled and subdued. But you have to stop waiting for it to fix itself. And you can't exclusively medicate it away.

If you think you might have SAD, do the boldest thing you can do—seek help. Get a professional in your corner. Learn the tools to fight back. And if professional help isn't an option right now? Then stick with me. Because no one—no one—is beyond improving their situation. Social anxiety wants you to believe you're stuck. I'm living proof it doesn't have to be that way.

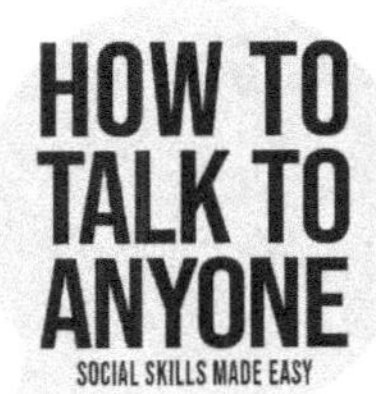

... Written by a naturally shy author who learned to overcome the overwhelming and painful symptoms of social anxiety through challenging negative self-talk and jumping head first into terrifying social situations.

Overcoming Fears About Socializing

I remember the moment I got thrown into the deep end of social anxiety. My church suddenly needed a new worship leader—someone who could play an instrument, sing, and lead a crowd of 200 every week. No one stepped up. I should've kept my head down, right? But for some reason, I raised my hand.

I had no idea what I was getting into. I wasn't a trained singer. I wasn't a confident performer. And every Sunday, like clockwork, the anxiety hit me like a sledgehammer. My hands would shake so badly I could barely play. My stomach turned itself inside out—I'd be physically sick before and after every service. I'd sweat through my clothes. My brain would blank out right when I needed it the most.

And every time, I thought to myself, "This is it. This is the moment I humiliate myself in front of everyone."

But here's what I learned: Anxiety is a liar. It tells you that fear means you're not ready. That discomfort means stop. That if you feel nervous, you're doing something wrong.

No. Fear is just the cost of admission. You don't wait for it to disappear. You act in spite of it.

And that's the mindset shift you will need to beat social anxiety. Whether you've been officially diagnosed with Social Anxiety Disorder or just feel like social situations drain the life out of you, here's the reality: there are tools—real, actionable tools—that can help. And I'm not talking about vague "just be yourself" advice. I'm talking about strategies that actually work. So, let's get to it.

Challenge your negative thoughts. Social anxiety makes you believe every worst-case scenario your brain throws at you. "You'll embarrass yourself." "They'll judge you." "You're not interesting." But here's the reality—most people aren't paying attention to you the way you think they are. They're too busy thinking about themselves. Next time that voice pipes up, challenge it. **Ask yourself: "Is this actually true?"** Most of the time, it's not. And once you start catching those lies, they lose their power.

Stop focusing on yourself. Have you ever noticed how, when you're anxious, your brain makes everything about you? "What if I mess up? What if they think I look ridiculous?" But guess what? Everyone else is feeling that way, too. Do yourself a favor. Flip it upside down. Instead, turn the focus outward. Be curious. **Ask people about their lives**. Dig into what makes them tick. They will breathe a sigh of relief, and so will you. The moment you stop obsessing over yourself, the pressure starts to drop.

And now for the big one: stop caring. This one might sound harsh, but it's a game-changer. Stop giving so much weight to every interaction, every outcome, every tiny detail. This doesn't mean you should be reckless or rude—it means giving yourself the freedom to exist without overanalyzing every move. **Social anxiety feeds off overthinking. So, interrupt the cycle.** Next time you feel those nerves creeping in, literally say, "I don't care." Say it out loud if you have to. Say it with as many expletives as it takes. Feel the weight drop. That moment of hesitation, that panic creeping in—kill it with three words: I don't care. Then do the thing anyway.

The more you practice these tools, the more you realize how freeing they can be.

Time for Some Action!

Try it. The next time your brain starts spiraling, hit it with "I don't care." See how it feels. Does it loosen the grip? Does it make that social pressure just a little less intense? Good. Because that's the goal.

Adopt healthy lifestyle habits. Now, let's talk about the basics. Your mind and body are a team—if one's struggling, the other suffers. So adopt healthy lifestyle habits. Eat well. Sleep enough. Get moving. You don't have to run marathons or survive on kale smoothies, but treating your body right makes a huge difference in how you handle stress.

Breathe. Sounds simple, but most people don't actually do it right. Shallow breathing fuels anxiety. And anxiety forces shallow breathing.

Deep, controlled breathing shuts it down. When you feel panic creeping in, take a slow breath in through your nose, hold it for a second, and let it out through your mouth. Feels better, right?

That's because oxygen is the antidote to anxiety.

Act confident, even if you don't feel it. Ever heard the phrase "fake it till you make it"? It's not a gimmick—it's psychology. Confidence isn't a personality trait; it's a skill. And the more you act confident, the more your brain starts believing it. Watch how confident people carry themselves and mirror it. Stand taller. Speak a little louder. Maintain eye contact. You might feel ridiculous at first, but give it time. One day, you'll realize you're not pretending anymore.

Be kind to yourself. You wouldn't rip apart a friend for feeling anxious, so why do it to yourself? If you make it to a social event but can't stay long, don't beat yourself up. Instead, acknowledge the win—you showed up. Progress is progress, no matter how small.

Ease into social situations. Don't throw yourself into a massive crowd right away. Start small. Some people will tell you to "go big or go home," but that's garbage advice when it comes to social anxiety. Instead of jumping into the deep end, wade in. Begin with situations that only trigger mild discomfort. Maybe it's grabbing coffee with one person instead of joining a loud dinner party. Maybe it's saying hi to a coworker before volunteering for a presentation. You build social confidence like a muscle—one rep at a time.

Face your fears. Social anxiety wants you to hide. The longer you avoid social situations, the scarier they become. Don't rip the Band-Aid off all at once, but stop making excuses. Take steps forward. The more you push through, the less power fear has over you.

Talk about it. Whether it's a therapist, a trusted friend, or a partner, saying your fears out loud strips them of their power. Sometimes, just voicing what's in your head makes it feel a little less big. And if the people in your life understand what you're dealing with, they can support you instead of unknowingly making it harder.

Ditch the crutches. Using alcohol, weed, or any other substance to get through an event might seem like an easy shortcut, but it's a trap. What starts as a "just this once" solution can turn into a dependency really fast. Plus, it doesn't actually fix the problem—it just delays it. Some readers will hate this advice. But don't you want to feel comfortable in social situations without needing something to take the edge off? Let the fear wash over you. Learn to observe it, feel it, and let it go. That means facing the discomfort head-on and owning it.

Take Massive Action!

Starting now, cut out one of your coping mechanisms for a week. Not your medicine. Just your self-prescribed crutch. No numbing. No hiding. Face the discomfort head-on. Feel it, let it envelop you, and watch as it loses its grip. Social anxiety isn't unbeatable. But you can't fight it if you keep giving it control. It's time to grow stronger than the noise.

Navigating Social Situations with Ease... Even When Anxiety Hits

You're at a party. A coworker introduces you to someone new. They ask, "So, what do you do?" And suddenly—nothing. Your brain takes a vacation. Words? Gone. Thoughts? Blank. Anxiety creeps in like a slow-motion car crash.

What do you do?

Here's the old you—panic. Fumble for words. Overthink every possible response. Maybe you blurt out something weird, maybe you laugh awkwardly, or maybe you escape to the nearest bathroom and stay there longer than necessary.

Now here's the new you. You have a plan. You're prepared. You've got strategies in your back pocket. And when that moment comes? You execute.

Pre-Game Rituals: Set Yourself Up for Success

You don't just wing it. You prep like a pro. Social confidence starts before you walk into the room.

Shake off the nerves. Anxiety builds in the body—so move. Do push-ups, stretch, or go for a quick walk before heading in. Motion kills stagnation.

Breathe with intention. Not shallow, panicked breaths—slow, deep, belly breaths. In for four, hold for four, out for four. Do this a few times before stepping in. Your body listens to your breathing.

Anchor yourself. Before walking into a room, remind yourself: "I belong here. I'm not proving anything. I'm just here to connect." Confidence isn't about being the best person in the room. It's about being present.

Lean on your people. Most of the time, loved ones want to help but have no clue what you need. Be direct. If you're walking into a situation that freaks you out, let a friend know how they can support you. Maybe you ask them to introduce you to people, or maybe you invent a predetermined signal if you need a breather. Clarity helps both of you. Walking into a social situation with backup can make all the difference.

How to Handle Awkward Silences Like a Pro

You're mid-conversation. Silence hits. Your brain screams: They're bored. You're boring. Shut that thought down. Silence isn't failure—it's a reset. Own it.

Option 1: Call it out. "Man, I completely lost my train of thought. What were we talking about?" Boom—human, relatable, and keeps the flow going.

Option 2: Pivot. "Anyway—random question. What's something cool you've been into lately?" Instant redirection, no awkwardness.

Option 3: Own the quiet. Confidence isn't about talking nonstop—it's about being so solid in yourself that you don't need to.

And if that silence still feels unbearable? Don't panic. Just reset.

Your Mid-Conversation Reset Trick

Anxiety spikes mid-conversation. Your brain starts running laps. Your focus drifts. You feel yourself withdrawing.

Here's what you do: Snap back into the moment with your senses.

Ground yourself. Feel your feet on the floor. Notice a color in the room. Take a sip of your drink and really taste it. This pulls you out of your head and back into "now".

Re-engage. Make a small physical shift—uncross your arms, lean in slightly, make eye contact. Then ask the person a question. Curiosity kills self-consciousness.

Worst-case scenario? Take a quick reset. Step outside, hit the restroom, breathe, regroup, and re-enter. No shame in a strategic retreat. The goal isn't perfection—it's resilience.

At the end of the day, social anxiety isn't a life sentence. It's a challenge—but one that you're more than capable of overcoming. The more you step into these situations with the right tools, the easier it gets. So no more sitting on the sidelines. No more overthinking your way out of experiences you actually want to have. You've got this. Now get out there and prove it to yourself.

Starting the Conversation and Actually Making It Fun

Alright, you made it. You pushed through the anxiety, walked into the event, and now you're standing there, scanning the room. You see someone interesting—maybe they're attractive, maybe they just have that energy. You want to talk to them. But instead of marching over and striking up a conversation, you freeze. That little voice creeps in:

"What if I say something dumb?"

"What if they think I'm boring?"

"What if I start talking and my brain just... stops working?"

First of all, stop. News flash: No one remembers the awkward small talk at a party. They remember confidence. So give them a reason to remember you. Let's break this down.

How to Actually Start the Conversation

Forget the idea that you need some genius opener. You're not delivering a TED Talk—you're just talking to another human being. Here's how NOT to do it:

Bad:

You: "So... uh... seen any good movies? Or, uh... bad ones?"

Them: "Yeah."

You: (awkward silence, panic sets in)

Now, here's how to do it right:

Better:

You: "What's the worst movie you've ever seen? The one that made you want to walk out of the theater?"

Them: [laughs, instantly engaged] "Oh man, let me tell you..."

Boom. Conversation flowing. Why? Because fun, unexpected questions make people think. They break the script. They make the moment memorable.

Other High-Impact Starters:

"What's something ridiculously small that you're weirdly passionate about?"

"If you had to be stuck in an elevator with one celebrity for five hours, who would you pick?"

"So, what's the most random way you've ever met a friend?"

The goal? Make it easy for them to engage. Generic questions lead to generic answers. If you want a conversation that doesn't feel like a job interview, ask better questions.

How to Keep the Conversation from Dying a Slow Death

So you've started talking. Great. But now what?

First, listen. Like, actually listen. Most people don't—because they're too busy planning what to say next. Don't be that person. Be present. When you listen, you pick up on things you can build on.

Example:

Them: "I just got back from a trip to Japan."

Bad response: "Oh, cool." [dead end]

Better response: "No way, what was the weirdest or best thing you ate there?"

Now you're in a real conversation. One that feels good, not forced.

Second, share your own stories. A conversation isn't an interrogation. If you just keep firing off questions, it gets weird. Bounce off their answers with your own experiences.

Them: "I tried this crazy sushi with sea urchin."

You: "That's wild. I had alligator once, but I feel like that doesn't even compare."

See what's happening? You're creating a rhythm. A back-and-forth. That's where the magic happens.

How to Escape Small Talk Hell

Sometimes, conversations drag. Maybe they're one-word answering you to death. Maybe you're just not vibing. Either way, you need an exit strategy—because nothing's worse than getting trapped in small talk purgatory.

The Smooth Exit Move:

Instead of awkwardly standing there waiting for the conversation to die, take control.

The callback exit: "Alright, I'm going to grab another drink, but before I go—tell me, was the sea urchin sushi actually good, or was it just a 'had to try it once' thing?"

The mission exit: "Hey, I need to go find my friend before they think I bailed, but it was great meeting you."

The bold move exit: "Alright, I feel like I just met my new go-to sushi critic. I'm definitely stealing your food recommendations."

It's confident. It's smooth. And it leaves the door open if you want to reconnect later.

Bottom Line: Make it easy, make it fun.

Conversations don't have to be high-pressure. Ditch the script, lean into curiosity, and remember—people don't remember every word you say. They remember how you made them feel. So show up, have fun, and own the moment. The goal was never to impress them with some grand closing statement—it was to make a genuine connection. If it clicks, great. If it doesn't, who cares? You took action. You got in the game. That's a win.

We've just tackled social anxiety head-on—what it is, where it comes from, how it grips you, and, more importantly, how to start breaking free from its hold. You've got the strategies. You've got the mindset shifts. Now, the real test begins: putting it into action.

But here's the thing—overcoming social anxiety isn't just about managing fear. It's about building something stronger in its place. That's where confidence and self-esteem come in. In the next chapter, we're not just talking about feeling good about yourself; we're talking about rewiring the way you see yourself so you can walk into any room, any situation, and own it. This is where you stop shrinking and start expanding. This is where you step up. Let's get to it.

***

Ending With a Bang!

Enough overthinking. If you want change, grab it—right now. Don't wait to 'feel ready.' Don't analyze it to death. Take action. Screw hesitation. Watch what happens. Here's your mission:

1. **Catch Your Negative Thoughts in the Act.** Every time that self-doubt creeps in, write it down. Look at it. Rip it apart. Ask yourself—is this actually true, or is it just fear talking? You'll be shocked at how many of your limiting beliefs crumble the second you challenge them.

2. **Flip the Script.** In your next conversation, stop obsessing over how you're coming across. Instead, make it your goal to learn something about the other person. Shift your focus outward. Get curious about them. The less you analyze yourself, the easier it gets.

3. **Act Like You Own the Room.** Confidence isn't a mood. It's a skill. Train it. Step into a situation that usually makes you anxious and act like you belong there. Shoulders back. Eye contact. Slow, deliberate movements. Then, afterward, take note of how different it felt. Because guess what? You just rewired a small part of your brain.

4. **Come Prepared.** Struggle with keeping a conversation going? Have three solid questions in your back pocket—something real, something engaging. But don't let them turn into a script. Be present. Listen. Adapt. The goal isn't to "perform" a conversation—it's to connect.

Confidence isn't built by thinking. It's built by doing. So stop waiting. Get out there and prove it.

Chapter 2 Recap: No More Hiding

- **Social anxiety isn't who you are.** It's just fear wearing a cheap disguise.

- **Every time you hide, you feed it.** When you act anyway, you kill it.

- **Your brain's fear wiring isn't permanent.** Challenge it. Break it. Rebuild it.

- **Confidence isn't gifted. It's earned.** Move first. Feel brave, second.

- **Screw perfection. Own the moment.** Connection beats looking flawless every time.

Takeaway:

Social anxiety doesn't own you unless you let it. Smash it. Drown it in action. Prove to yourself you're bigger than your fear.

Chapter 3

Approach Like You Matter

I didn't just want to survive social situations any longer. I wanted to enjoy them.

I was committed to finding that confidence—even if it meant trial and error—because I knew what was waiting on the other side: peace, clarity, and calm in my inner storm.

Confidence turns approaching people into second nature. Speaking up stops feeling risky and starts feeling like a thrill. If confidence were easy, everyone would have it, right?

Building confidence is relatively simple, but it isn't easy. Self-doubt, negative self-talk, and that nasty little demon called *imposter syndrome* will do everything in their power to keep you in the shadows. And guess what? Even some of the most successful people on the planet have battled these same demons.

Tom Hanks, a two-time Academy Award winner. Lady Gaga, a chart-topping musician with 13 Grammys. Maria Shriver, an Emmy-winning journalist and best-selling author. On paper, they're the best of the best. And yet, every one of them has admitted to feeling like a fraud.

Self-Doubt Is A Habit

Gina Vild, a writer for *Psychology Today*, knows this feeling all too well. She laid it all out in her article, **"How I Cured Myself of Imposter Syndrome—Three Steps to Eliminate Fear of Being 'Too Much' and 'Not Enough.'"**

Gina was a young professional, packed with potential but carrying a relentless, nagging voice inside her head telling her she was an imposter. It didn't matter what she achieved—self-doubt loomed over every success like a dark cloud, convincing her she was just one step away from being "found out."

Then came the moment that changed everything.

She went on a date with a guy she saw as out of her league—sophisticated, accomplished. Someone who'd eventually figure out she wasn't "enough." So, before he could reject her, she beat him to it, trying to set him up with her friend instead.

But instead of taking the bait, he looked her in the eye and listed all the reasons why he was charmed by her.

That's when it hit her—maybe she wasn't the fraud she thought she was. Maybe, just maybe, she needed to reshape her thoughts and start seeing herself the way others saw her.

From that night forward, Gina committed to silencing the imposter syndrome voice in her head. She dove into self-discovery, built a trusted inner circle for honest feedback, and started viewing failure as nothing more than a stepping stone. Slowly but surely, she pried imposter syndrome's grip off her life and began stepping forward with confidence and authenticity.

Her story is proof that self-doubt isn't truth. It's just a bad habit in a loud costume. And like any habit, it can be broken. But only if you do something about it. Gina changed the game on imposter syndrome. Confidence doesn't show up just because you wish for it. It comes when you make a move—when you take risks, challenge your thoughts, and show yourself that you belong.

Let's get to work.

ENGINE 1: THE MIND GAME

Confidence begins with fixing the voice in your head. If that voice is tearing you down, your other efforts will crash and burn.

Welcome to **Engine 1: The Mind Game**.

This is where you learn to interrupt the toxic loops. To rewire your thoughts. To train your brain to fight for you, not against you.

Building and Keeping Bulletproof Confidence

When do you feel like a fraud? What triggers it? Write it down. Find the patterns. The faster you recognize imposter syndrome's script, the faster you can rewrite it.

Because here's the deal—if you don't confront these thoughts, they'll run the show. And you? You're too amazing to let that happen.

Confidence isn't loud. It's not perfection. It's trust.

It's knowing that even without all the answers, you'll find your way.

That's real strength—showing up when it's scary, chasing your goals, taking risks, stepping up anyway.

According to *Verywell Mind* (2024), confidence can be a general sense of control over your life or situation-specific, meaning you might be a rockstar in one area but a nervous wreck in another. The good news? Confidence is a skill, and skills can be learned.

And let's be real. The benefits of confidence are endless. It reduces stress, strengthens mental health, and keeps you steady when life throws curveballs. It helps you communicate clearly, hold your own in conversations, and be taken seriously, whether at work or in your personal life.

Verywell Mind (2024) also notes, *"The doubt that comes with second-guessing yourself has internal and external repercussions. Confidence affects how you feel about yourself and communicates to others that you are trustworthy and capable—which can be helpful socially and at work."*

Translation? The way you see yourself directly affects how others see you.

If you walk into a room believing you don't belong, people pick up on that energy. But when you own your presence, when you carry yourself like someone who deserves to be there, suddenly, people start seeing you differently.

Because if you don't believe in yourself—even just a little—your brain will do everything in its power to keep you stuck. So before you can build confidence, you need to get your mind on board.

Find Your Why

Why do you want confidence? And don't give some half-hearted answer. Be honest. Is it to build a career you're actually excited about? To stop feeling like a side character in your own life? To finally connect with people on a deeper level? When you know **why** you want it, that reason will carry you through every doubt, every fear, and every moment of hesitation. According to *Psychology Today* (2023), "What your why is, remind yourself of it because it will motivate you through any moments of doubt and make you even more passionate." You don't build confidence because it sounds nice—you build it because something inside you **demands it.**

Be Open to a Fresh Approach

Your brain is a master at running its mouth. Sometimes, it's your hype man. Sometimes, it's your biggest enemy—feeding you doubt, fear, and made-up disasters. If you don't take control, that noise will run your life.

Start fresh:

Forgive yourself.

Stop letting your job or status define you.

Choose grace over guilt.

Confidence grows when you stop replaying your flaws and start recognizing your strengths.

Now, you can begin to take a fresh look around and notice the weeds that have grown up in your mental garden while you weren't paying attention.

Weed 1: Overthinking Yourself into Shipwreck

If you've ever found yourself replaying a conversation from three years ago or spiraling over some minor mistake that no one else even remembers, congratulations—you're human. But overthinking is a confidence killer. It magnifies the meaningless.

Overthinking turns shadows into monsters. Most of the time, you're not solving anything. You're only spiraling. If you want confidence, you've got to call this out for what it is: a waste of energy. You'll learn how to shut it down in Engine 2. For now, just notice when and how often your brain obsesses over problems that don't exist.

Weed 2: Recognize What's Dragging You Down

What situations make you feel small? What experiences trigger self-doubt? To stop letting these things lurk in the background, you must call them out.

Ask yourself: *Do these things actually deserve the power they have over me?* You get to decide what defines you. And guess what? Most of the stuff weighing you down shouldn't even be in the equation.

Weed 3: Negativity

A lot of people think being hard on themselves is necessary for success. They use negative self-talk as a twisted kind of motivation, thinking it'll push them to do better.

Reality check: That's garbage.

Negative reinforcement doesn't build confidence—it destroys it. It keeps you in a constant state of *I'm not good enough*, which makes you hesitate, second-guess, and hold back. It makes you worse, not better.

The truth is, people don't perform at their best when they're constantly berated—even if the voice doing the berating is their own. Encouragement wins. Positive self-talk isn't about pretending everything is perfect. Remember that it's about giving yourself the same kind of support you'd give to a friend.

Before you tear yourself down again, ask: *Would I say this to someone I care about?* If the answer is no, then don't say it to yourself.

Your thoughts aren't facts. Just because your brain **delivers them with passion and absolute certainty doesn't make them true**. Most of the time? It's fear pretending to be logic. In Engine 2, you'll learn exactly how to shut that voice down and replace it with something that actually serves you. For now, just notice it—and don't default to believing what it is telling you.

Once you start observing that cycle, self-doubt naturally begins losing its grip. And that awareness? It's your opening bell to step into the ring.

So what's the next move?

Train your mind like a fighter in the ring. Guard up. Eyes sharp. Hit back when fear swings. Confidence is built in every mental round you choose to win.

Personal Reflection

Name the Voice: Pick one negative thought that keeps plaguing your mind. Ask yourself, "Where did this come from? Whose voice is it, really?" Name it. Write it down. Because if you don't call it out, it keeps calling the shots unchallenged.

ENGINE 2: THE ACTION LAYER

Engine 1 found the weeds in your mind garden. But now it's time to get rid of them.

Welcome to **Engine 2: The Action Layer**.

This is where you start taking active control over harmful thoughts through practice. It's not just about moving—it's about moving with intention.

This is where you disrupt the spiral, break the loop, and put belief to work.

Confidence gets forged in friction, not fantasy. You can't merely decide to be confident; you must prove to yourself that you **deserve** to be confident. And that happens one step at a time. Small, manageable goals will get you there faster than one giant, paralyzing leap. Every single win—no matter how minor—adds up. That moment when you push past hesitation and speak up? A win. That time you introduce yourself instead of waiting to be noticed? Another win. Stack them up, and suddenly, you're operating on a whole new level. Celebrate each victory. **You're not "trying." You're training.**

Building Unshakeable Confidence One Step at a Time

Disrupt the Loop—Fast

Your mind is on autopilot, but you're the pilot. Time to grab the controls. Those negative loops? They're just well-worn ruts. Mental habits, not truth.

When that voice kicks in with its usual routine—*You're not good enough. Everyone thinks you're awkward.*—shut it down. Interrupt it. Say "stop" out loud if you have to. Blast your favorite song. Do anything that forces your brain to hit pause.

Then, instead of letting your thoughts spiral, give yourself space. You don't have to fix everything at the moment. Sometimes, you only need to step back, breathe, and let your emotions settle before you decide what's real and what's simply your mind talking trash. ***But don't stop there.***

Reframe the Tracks

Once you stop the runaway train of self-doubt, it's time to rebuild the tracks.

Here's the thing—stopping the thought isn't enough. If you leave an empty space, your brain will fill it with more of the same self-doubt. That's why **replacement works better than suppression**. Instead of just shutting down the thought, you need to swap it out for something stronger. Something that works for you instead of against you.

This isn't about lying to yourself. It's about giving your mind a better script to follow.

Plan your comebacks.

If your self-talk says: *I'm terrible at socializing. People think I'm awkward.* The reframe is: *I'm learning to be more confident, and every interaction is progress.*

If your self-talk says: *I'll never be good at this.*
The reframe is: *I've overcome challenges before. Why should this be any different?*

Every time your mind starts playing the old script, hit it with the new one.

Turn Positive Thinking into a Habit

What you say to yourself matters. If your inner dialogue is trash—constant self-doubt, negative self-talk, and worst-case scenario thinking—then guess what? You're going to feel like trash. But the mind is trainable. The more you tell yourself something, the more your brain starts to believe it.

Daily affirmations aren't some cheesy self-help gimmick. They're a system reboot. Science backs it. Your brain starts to believe what it hears on repeat.

And this isn't a one-time fix. Confidence isn't built by thinking something once. It's built by repeating it until it becomes your new default.

So, make it a new habit. Your mind's going to talk anyway, so you'd better make sure it's saying something that serves you.

Positive thinking isn't fluff. It's fuel. It's not about pretending life is perfect—it's about keeping your head right when it isn't.

Every morning, feed your mind what it needs. Out loud. On paper. In the mirror. Doesn't matter. Just make it real.

Try this to start:

> *"I can do this. I don't need permission."*
> *"I'm not waiting to be ready. I'm already enough."*
> *"I've made it through worse. I'll make it through this."*
> *"The more I try, the more I grow. I'm built for progress."*

Feed your brain that kind of ammo every day. Because when doubt shows up—and it will—you need something stronger to fire back.

Train your inner voice to fight for you, not against you. That's not wishful thinking. That's how you win the day.

The goal? Automatic confidence. A default setting that isn't rooted in fear, doubt, or hesitation but in self-belief and truth.

And the only way to get there? Put in the reps.

Take Massive Action!

The Mindset Reset Challenge: Pick one negative thought that keeps showing up like it pays rent in your head. Now follow the four steps below and rewire it on the spot. No excuses. It's time to serve that thought an eviction notice and replace it with something that actually builds you.

1. **Catch It** – Notice the self-doubt. Don't justify it. Only name it.

2. **Challenge It** – Ask: Is this fear, or is this fact? Make it prove itself.

3. **Change It** – Reframe the story. Choose a better thought.

4. **Repeat It** – Positive thinking isn't magic. It is repetition. Build the habit.

Remember Your Wins—And Keep a Record

Your brain loves to focus on failures. It's wired for survival, which means it clings to every moment of embarrassment, every misstep, every awkward encounter. You must retrain it. Start keeping track of your wins. Think back to times when you faced a challenge and crushed it. Times you stepped up. Moments you did the thing even when it scared you. Write them down. Use them as fuel. Just like a scientist builds a case with evidence, you need to build a case for your own capability. You are not your doubts—you are the sum of every moment you've pushed past them.

Surround Yourself with the Right People

Confidence thrives in the right environment. Negative people drain it faster than anything else. They'll tell you what you can't do, that you're not good enough, that you should "stay realistic." Warn them, and if necessary, cut them loose. Constructive feedback is one thing—constant discouragement is another. Build your circle with people who want you to win. People who push you, challenge you, and see your potential before you even do.

Protect Your Self-Esteem

Self-esteem isn't just a "feel-good" buzzword. It's your foundation. When you respect yourself, everything changes—how you walk, how you speak, how you choose.

But if you keep treating yourself like you don't matter? Don't be surprised when the world starts agreeing with you.

That's how confidence crumbles—when you hand your value to everyone but yourself.

Stop waiting for someone else to say you matter.

Show up like you belong. Speak like you matter.

Because when you move through life with self-respect, people notice. And more importantly, you notice (*Mayo Clinic*, 2024).

ENGINE 3: PROJECT POWER

You've rewired your thoughts and stacked the reps. Now it's time to show the world what you've built.

This is **Engine 3: Project Power**.

Confidence doesn't live in flashes of action. It lives in how you carry yourself daily. In how you treat your body, your time, your energy.

This section is about making your confidence visible. Not faking it. Not forcing it. Just showing up like someone who belongs—because you do.

It's about broadcasting belief until your body catches up. Train your posture, voice, and energy, and the world starts responding to the real you.

Project Confidence Like a Pro

The world reacts to what you project, and if you come across as confident, capable, and self-assured, people will treat you that way. That's why projecting confidence is a game-changer.

Studies show that people who appear confident get more opportunities, build stronger relationships, and navigate life with far less resistance. It's not magic—it's human psychology. We naturally trust people who carry themselves as if they know what they're doing. We listen to people who speak like they have something worth saying. Confidence attracts.

And here's the best part: You don't have to **feel** it to **project** it. You can train yourself to look confident first, and soon enough, your brain will catch up. I call this the "confidence override". You use posture, tone, and attitude to broadcast confidence outwardly until your mind starts believing it inwardly. It's a hack that rewires your entire presence.

How I Accidentally Found My Mojo

At the beginning of the chapter, I told you how I spent years trapped in my own head—shy, nervous, and convinced that everyone around me could see right through me. My body language screamed, "weak, vulnerable, awkward." I'd hunch my shoulders, tuck my chin, and do everything possible to take up less space. The problem? That posture wasn't hiding me. It was highlighting my insecurity.

And when people noticed? That only made it worse. More attention meant more self-consciousness, which meant more awkwardness. A vicious cycle.

Then, one day, I decided to flip things entirely. Counterintuitively. I decided I'd stop trying to just "fit in" and started owning the moment like I was superhuman.

I didn't fake confidence—I acted as if I had no choice but to be unstoppable. Instead of struggling to be "normal," I would carry myself like the most powerful person in the room. The result? People treated me that way. And soon, I started believing it myself.

And guess what? It worked!

The second I adjusted my posture, my energy shifted. My shoulders squared, my head lifted, and my body stopped trying to shrink. Suddenly, people responded to me differently. They treated me like I belonged, like I had something to say—because I acted like I did.

And here's where things got interesting. I actually started believing it. My fake confidence grew into real confidence. That small shift in how I carried myself rewired how I saw myself.

That's the trick: Don't aim for "average" when you feel stuck. Stop blending in. If you're buried deep in self-doubt, sometimes you have to overcorrect to break free. I had to convince myself that I was powerful before I could naturally own it.

Eventually, I no longer needed my superhuman mindset—I just became the confident person I had pretended to be.

Confidence When You Don't Feel It

Your body tells a story before you ever open your mouth. Walk into a room hunched over, eyes down, energy small? People subconsciously see weakness before you even speak. But control your energy and presentation? You become a person of authority. That's the power of body language.

Confidence is part psychology, part body language, part communication. You don't have to master everything at once, but if you start with these techniques, you'll immediately notice a difference in how people respond to you and how you feel about yourself.

And while you are reading this book to learn to talk to anyone, confidence starts before you say a word. Your body's talking whether you mean it to or not. So train it to speak strength.

Start with your eyes. Dodge eye contact, and you'll come off as unsure or invisible. Lock it in, and people feel your presence.

Straighten up. Shoulders back. Chin up. No slouching, no shrinking. You're not asking for permission to exist. You're claiming space.

Lean in. Literally. Confidence doesn't pull back. It moves toward. Show interest. Get close enough to be heard, seen, and felt.

Get your hands out of your pockets. Nervous hands hide. Confident ones move naturally, emphasizing your words and keeping people engaged.

Don't cross anything. Not your arms. Not your legs. Not your hands in front like you're guarding treasure. Crossed-up posture screams one thing: I don't feel safe. And people pick up on it subconsciously.

Stillness is power. Fidgeting screams fear. Control your movement, and you control the room.

Now, walk like you mean it. You're not tiptoeing through life. Long strides. Solid posture. You own the ground you walk on.

That first handshake? It's not small talk—it's your introduction to the room. Weak, limp, forgettable? You've already lost ground.

A solid handshake says, "I'm here. I'm steady." I've got weight. That grip tells the other person, without a word, that you're someone worth paying attention to.

And once you're in the conversation? Watch what happens when you mirror someone's energy. I'm not talking about mimicry—I'm talking about subtly reflecting the other person's posture and gestures. It builds instant connection and trust.

Lean in when they lean in. Match their tone. Reflect their posture. People trust those who feel familiar. You build rapport not with words but with rhythm.

Then comes the voice. You don't rush it. You don't fill silence with noise. You own the pause. Confident people don't just speak clearly. They let their words breathe.

Every sentence you say is a declaration.

You slow your roll. You let the silence land. That's presence. That's power.

But don't forget to relax yourself. Tension betrays you. Your jaw is clenched, your shoulders are locked, and you don't even notice.

Take a second. Breathe. Loosen up. That simple act changes how you look, how you sound, and how people respond.

Finally, speak like your voice has roots. No mumbling. No fading out. Say what you mean and stand behind it.

Don't try too hard. You are enough.

You want people to believe in you? Start by sounding like you believe in yourself.

Know what you stand for—and don't back down.

What do you believe in? What do you value? If you don't have answers, go back to your answers in Chapter 1—because your beliefs and values are your foundation. They're what hold you steady when life throws punches. They guide your decisions, shape your actions, and give you a rock-solid core to stand on. Without them, you're just floating, letting the world dictate who you are.

Confidence isn't about looking the part. It's about knowing yourself so well that nothing shakes you. If you stand for something, you don't get thrown off by every challenge or criticism. You move through life with purpose, direction, and certainty.

So dig deep. What do you really care about? What's non-negotiable for you? What lines will you never cross? As you recognize your values, live them. Confidently. The world respects people who stand firm in who they are. More importantly, you'll respect yourself.

Step Up and Own Your Expertise

Let's get real. You already know a lot more than you give yourself credit for. But if you don't own it, people won't see it.

The skills you've built over time? The experience you carry? That's value. That's leverage. But most people—especially those struggling with confidence—downplay what they know. They hesitate. They shrink. They act like they're just "figuring things out," while less qualified people boldly step up and take the opportunities.

Here's the deal: stop playing small. If you know something, say it. If you have experience, share it. If you have a skill, use it. People respect confidence, and confidence isn't arrogance. It's clarity. It's knowing what you bring and not being afraid to step up when it matters.

Next time you feel the urge to shrink—don't. Speak up. Stand firmly. Own your space.

Stop Squirming at Compliments

Taking compliments should be the easiest thing in the world. Someone tells you something good about yourself, and all you have to do is say, "Thanks."

But what do most people do? They deflect. They brush it off, downplay it, or throw a compliment right back as if they can't possibly deserve one themselves.

Enough of that. Stop rejecting what you've earned.

When someone compliments you, believe them. They're seeing something in you that you might not even see in yourself yet. If someone tells you you're talented, capable, strong, or impressive, accept it. They're not lying. They're not mistaken. They're simply seeing the version of you that you're still learning to recognize.

Confidence means standing in your value—not dodging it. So next time someone compliments you, hold your head up, look them in the eye, and just say, "Thank you."

No excuses. No self-deprecating jokes. You're not "being polite." You're stepping into your power. And power doesn't apologize for existing.

Because the second you start believing in your strengths, the world will, too.

Confidence isn't luck. It's not something some people are born with, and others aren't. It's a skill, and like any skill, it can be learned, practiced, and mastered.

The secret? Act first. Feel later.

If you move like you're confident, stand like you're confident, and speak like you're confident, your brain will catch up. The shift happens faster than you think.

Confidence isn't about never feeling doubt. It's about pressing forward anyway, with your head high, your voice steady, and your presence undeniable.

Start now. Adjust your posture. Hold eye contact. Speak with certainty.

Then watch how people—and your own mind—start treating you differently.

Take Massive Action!

Command the Space: Today, walk into a room like you were born to lead it. Shoulders back, eyes up, voice steady. Don't say anything. Make eye contact with three people—and hold it a beat longer than usual. Notice how it feels. What part of you squirms inside? What part of you loves it?

Confidence Over the Long Haul

Confidence is a lifestyle. It's how you treat yourself when no one's watching.

Otherwise, you might feel unstoppable for a day and then go right back to self-doubt. No, real confidence sticks when you build a lifestyle that supports it.

That's where most people fall short. They do the mental work, maybe push themselves socially a little, but then? They neglect the foundation. They let exhaustion, self-criticism, and comparison creep in like termites, eating away at everything they've built.

You can't let that happen. If you want lasting confidence, the kind that doesn't crumble when life throws you a curveball, then you've got to start treating yourself like someone worth taking care of. That means fueling your mind and body the right way, shutting down the toxic habit of measuring yourself against others, and making space for the things that actually make you feel alive.

Let's get into it. Because if you want to stand strong, you've got to build your foundation right.

Take Care of Yourself Like It Matters

You want to feel like a force to be reckoned with? Start treating yourself like one. Confidence isn't just a mental game—it's a full-body commitment. How you eat, sleep, move, and recover impacts how you show up in the world. If you're running on fumes, surviving on garbage food, and neglecting your own well-being, don't expect to feel strong when you need to.

Get some sleep. Feed your body real fuel. Get healthy. Because when you take care of yourself, you start carrying yourself differently. Stack the deck in your favor.

Stop Comparing. Focus on You.

I'll preach this sermon over and over. There's only one way to lose before you even start: constantly measuring yourself against someone else.

Everyone's journey is different. Everyone's challenges are unique. You don't know what battles someone else is fighting, just like they don't know yours. So why waste time examining your progress against their highlight reel?

The only person you need to be better than is the person you were yesterday. That's it. Focus on your own path. Every win, no matter how small, is still a win. Every step forward counts. Keep moving. Keep growing. Keep building yourself into the person you want to be on your own terms.

Do What You Love. Don't Resist the Unknown.

You know what gives you confidence? Doing things you're good at. Mastering a skill, owning your craft, feeling like a savage in your element. So, lean into the things that light you up. Build on your strengths.

But don't stop there. Confidence isn't just built in the familiar—it's forged in the unknown. Step outside your comfort zone. Try something new. Be willing to suck at it. Because the real power move? Becoming someone who thrives in uncertainty. That's how you turn confidence into something unshakable.

You won't love every new thing. You won't be great at all of them. That's not the point. The point is, you tried. You expanded. You proved to yourself that you can handle new experiences, new challenges, and new conversations with people you haven't met yet.

Confidence isn't about knowing you'll always win. It's about knowing you'll be fine, no matter what happens.

The Next Level: Turning Confidence Into Connection

You've put in the work to trust yourself. You've started to shake off the negativity, the doubt, the comparison traps. You're learning that no one is coming to hand you confidence. You have to take it.

So, here's the ongoing challenge: In the next conversations you have—whether with a friend, a coworker, or a stranger—I want you to own them. Make eye contact. Speak like you mean it. Stand like you deserve to be there. No more shrinking. No more hesitation. Just presence.

Now, let's take it further.

In the next few chapters, we're getting out of our heads and moving into real-world application. Part 2 is all about social skills—developing, refining, and mastering them. Confidence is the foundation, but conversation? That's where the magic happens.

So, get ready to level up. Because embracing your worth is one thing. Next, it's about being present and leading the interaction well.

Let's get cracking!

***

Ending With a Bang!

You've made it this far—now it's time to lock it in. Confidence isn't built by waiting. It's built by doing. The faster you take action, the faster you see results. So don't just read this. Live it. Right now.

1. **Rewire Your Inner Dialogue:** Your mind is either your greatest weapon or your biggest enemy—it all depends on how you train it. Every morning, swap out the negativity for a power statement. Tell yourself exactly what you need to hear: "I've got this. I belong here. I can handle whatever comes my way." Speak it, believe it, and watch how your mindset starts shifting.

2. **Make Self-Reflection a Habit:** If you don't take time to evaluate your growth, you'll stay stuck in the same cycle. Start reflecting on your wins, your struggles, and what each experience is teaching you. If you need a system to lock this in, grab my free **Daily Confidence-Building Exercises Guided Journal.** It's selling on Amazon, but you can download it for free right now. Use it. Learn from it. Build from it.   Free download: https://posg.life/FreeDCBE or Purchase hard copy: https://posg.life/BuyDailyConfidence

3. **Master Your Confident Stance:** Your body sends a message before you ever open your mouth. What's yours saying? Stand tall. Shoulders back, chin up, solid eye contact. Pick your confident power pose and practice it until it's second nature. When you walk into a room, let them feel your presence before you even say a word.

Chapter 3 Recap: Approach Like You Matter

- Confidence transforms doubt into opportunity, making social interactions thrilling rather than terrifying.

- Everyone, even celebrities like Tom Hanks and Lady Gaga, battles imposter syndrome; overcoming it starts with reframing our thoughts.

- Confidence is built on trust in oneself, not on being perfect or all-knowing. It grows from actions, not just desires.

- It's forged through resilience, understanding that failure is not a setback but a setup for a comeback.

- Protecting self-esteem and stopping the cycle of negative self-talk is crucial for sustaining confidence.

Takeaway:

Confidence is built. It's about trusting your power to conquer challenges, not just in smooth times but when the going gets rough. It's standing tall in your beliefs, regardless of where you stand. Ignite it now, take bold steps, and watch how you revolutionize not only your self-view but how the world sees you.

Part II
Power Tools to Talk to Anyone

Chapters 4 – 6

"Effective communication is about more than just exchanging information. It's about understanding the emotion and intentions behind the information."–Lawrence Robinson, Jeanne Segal, Melinda Smith

Many people stumble through conversations—awkward, anxious, unsure of what to say or how to say it. They rely on small talk, miss the cues, and wonder why nothing sticks.

Not you. Not anymore.

This is where we burn it to the ground. These chapters don't hand you tips. They forge you into what this book promised: someone who can talk to anyone. You'll use chit-chat as a launch ramp to real presence. You'll listen so sharply it disarms people. And you'll communicate volumes without saying a word.

Small talk becomes soul talk. Words start to matter. And every room you walk into? You'll walk in ready to lead.

This isn't about tricks or hacks. It's about becoming the kind of person who owns your voice, speaks with purpose, and makes an impression that sticks without forcing it.

Get in. Get open. Get real. It's time to make your communication unforgettable.

Chapter 4

From Small Talk to Soul Talk

Conversation is an art form—and most people are finger painting blindfolded.

They mumble through small talk. Ramble without purpose. Walk away from every interaction, wondering, "Why can't I connect? Why don't they listen?"

Meanwhile, every opportunity they want—every friendship, every job offer, every spark of belonging—is slipping through the cracks.

But not for you. Not anymore.

You're here to master the one skill that changes everything. The ability to turn a few words into a moment that lands. That impacts. That makes people lean in, listen, and remember your name.

Because when you can talk to anyone—with presence, with purpose, with fire—you stop being overlooked. You stop being underestimated. And you start building relationships that open doors, shift rooms, and change your life.

This chapter is your turning point. Let's build your social masterpiece—and make every word count.

Annalisa Barbieri discovered this skill. She grew up in a house full of noise but no connection. Her mother and the neighbor, Pam, fired off words like bullets—cutting each other off, hijacking stories, talking just to be heard. Not a moment of silence. Not a second of real listening. The conversations were loud. But they were hollow.

And Annalisa felt it.

She caught on early: talking and connecting weren't the same. She watched people speak for hours and walk away with nothing new. No insight. No bond. Just chatter.

Later, as an advice columnist for *The Guardian*, that childhood echo slammed back even harder. Letters poured in from people desperate to be understood yet unable to communicate what they really felt.

That's when it hit her: it's not the talking that brings people closer. It's the kind of listening that says, "I'm with you."

So, she flipped the rules. She stopped talking to respond and started listening to understand. Not just with her ears—with her full presence. Her tone softened. Her questions cut deeper. People opened up like never before. She didn't just hear them. She got them.

Everything shifted from that moment forward.

And why should this matter to you?

Maybe you're thinking, I don't see why this is important. Why do I need this? Simple. Conversation isn't about charm, wit, and clever statements. It's about connection. And connection is everything. Friendships. Careers. Influence. Trust.

When you know how to connect, people remember you. Respect you. Follow you. That's power.

This chapter isn't about sounding smart—it's about making people feel something. You'll learn to start conversations that matter, take them deeper, and leave every interaction stronger than you found it.

No charisma required. Just practice.

Let's get tactical.

How to Start Meaningful Conversations

Think about it. Most conversations? They're forgettable. Quick hellos, passing comments, surface-level chit-chat. But the conversations that stick—the ones that actually mean something—go deeper.

A meaningful conversation is more than words filling a void. It's a level-up from small talk, the kind of exchange where you walk away knowing something new about them, about yourself, about the world (Psyche, 2024).

When you master meaningful conversation, you create real connections. You build relationships that aren't just casual but genuine. You gain a deeper understanding of people, which makes you better at reading social dynamics. And when you truly connect with someone, you create a space where they feel comfortable being open, honest, and real.

So, what does a meaningful conversation actually look like? It's built on three things: openness, engagement, and mutual respect. The best conversations make people feel wanted and encouraged to share without fear of judgment. When that happens, people open up, barriers come down, and the connection deepens.

You're here to be different. Magical. Meaningful.

Want to make that happen? Here's how.

Starting Meaningful Conversations

Meaningful conversation is a skill. You don't get there by winging it. You get there by being intentional. By asking better questions, listening harder, and giving people a clear, honest spotlight that says, "You matter."

So what does "meaningful" actually mean?

It means people feel safe to be themselves. It means no one's posturing or performing. It means they feel heard, not handled. Valued, not sized up.

The best conversations aren't about being clever. They're about creating space for truth.

Here's how you lead that kind of exchange:

Start with Real Questions

Surface questions get surface answers. "Did you have a good weekend?" gets you a shrug. "What was the highlight of your weekend?" gets you a story. Real connection starts with real curiosity. Ask like you mean it. Listen like you care. That's how people open up. We'll hit that harder in a minute.

Make Space for Everyone

Great conversations are team sports. If someone's stuck on the sidelines, pull them in. "What's your take?" "I'd love to hear your thoughts." One simple nudge can shift the whole dynamic. Inclusion isn't just polite; it's powerful. It turns background players into bold voices and transforms forgettable chatter into unforgettable connection.

Lead with "For Me…"

Want to keep a conversation from turning combative? Lead with "For me…"

You're not preaching—you're sharing perspective. That one shift drops defenses, shows respect, and keeps the energy open. It's not about winning. It's about being heard and hearing back.

Actually Respond

Most people fake listening—nodding, then hijack the conversation. Don't be that person. If someone shares something, don't steamroll past it. Pause. Respond. Then, get curious.

Try: "No way—how'd that happen?" or "That must've been tough. What was that like?"

It's not just about asking a question. It's the follow-up that builds the bridge.

Be First to Go First

You want honesty? Connection? Trust? Go first. Say something real. It doesn't need to be heavy—just true.

"I tried something way outside my comfort zone this weekend—ever done that?"

Vulnerability invites vulnerability. Boldness follows. You set the tone.

That's the difference between small talk and real connection. One fades fast. The other leaves a mark.

And this? This is just the warm-up. Now, let's make sure we hone those skills needed to open the conversation in a way that invites depth.

Your Arsenal: Powerful Conversation Starters

It's critical to ask questions that use small talk to spark something real. The kind that light people up, crack them open, and make them say, "Nobody's ever asked me that before."

The people who seem like naturals at connection? They're not lucky. They're strategic. They know how to lead with curiosity, and that's what makes them magnetic.

You don't need charm. You need the right tools to shift the energy from vague to invested.

Here are two go-to arsenals—one for professional settings and one for personal connections. Keep them ready. Use them wisely. Watch what happens.

20 Conversation Starters for Professional Settings

Small talk is the doorway. These questions kick it wide open. Whether you're networking, interviewing, or just building rapport at work, this list turns cheap filler into fuel—conversations that build trust, reveal insight, and leave a lasting impression.

> 1. What inspired you to pursue your current career?
>
> 2. What's your go-to strategy for solving tough problems?
>
> 3. What's been your biggest challenge at work recently?
>
> 4. What's the work project you're most proud of?
>
> 5. What keeps you motivated when things get tough?
>
> 6. What's your best productivity hack?

7. What's the best way to give constructive feedback?

8. What's one professional development goal you're working on right now?

9. What's the best team you've ever worked with, and why?

10. How do you balance work and life without burning out?

11. What's the single most important skill in this industry?

12. How do you stay focused and avoid distractions?

13. What's your approach to networking and building professional relationships?

14. What's your favorite part of your job?

15. How do you handle workplace conflict in a way that actually works?

16. What leadership principle guides your biggest decisions?

17. What advice would you give to someone just starting in this field?

18. If you had to switch careers tomorrow, what would you do?

19. What's a hidden skill or talent you have that most people don't know about?

20. What industry do you think is about to blow up in the next ten years?

Pick one of these, and suddenly, you're not just another face in the crowd. You're someone people actually want to talk to.

20 Conversation Starters for Personal Relationships

Stronger friendships, tighter families, real relationships all start with better questions. These aren't icebreakers. They're invitations to something real.

1. What's your most cherished memory?

2. What's something that always brings you joy?

3. What's one thing you've always wanted to try but haven't yet?

4. What's the first childhood memory that comes to mind?

5. Would you call yourself an introvert, extrovert, or something in between?

6. What's your favorite thing about yourself?

7. How have your priorities shifted over the last five years?

8. If you could either travel to space or back in time, which would you choose?

9. If your life were a book, what would the title be?

10. How do you push through self-doubt when it creeps in?

11. What's the biggest lesson failure has ever taught you?

12. How do you personally define respect?

13. What's a childhood vacation that still sticks with you?

14. Who has had the biggest influence on shaping who you are today?

15. What does the word "home" mean to you?

16. If you had to pick, would you rather be rich or incredibly intelligent?

17. What's something you've done recently that made you proud?

18. Where do you think society will be in 100 years?

19. What's an unpopular opinion you have?

20. How do you define adventure?

These aren't just questions. They're conversation igniters. They take you from surface-level small talk to real human connection. The magic isn't in having the list. It's in knowing when to use it.

Start light. Read the room. Then, when the moment opens, drop a question that flips the script. That's how you stop blending in and start standing out.

People don't crave more noise. They crave something real. Give it to them, and they'll remember you.

This isn't about memorizing lines. It's about building instinct.

So next time the conversation falls flat, don't tap out. Lean in. Ask deeper. Listen closer. Create a moment, and watch what opens up.

Turn Small Talk into Real Talk

You hooked the whale. Your opening question landed. Now comes the real test. Can you keep the line tight and reel them in?

Pull too hard, too fast? You lose them.

Don't pull at all? They drift.

That's where most people blow it. They start strong, then stall out in the shallow end of small talk.

Let's fix that.

They responded to your opening question… now what?

Remember that small talk isn't the enemy. It's the warm-up. The problem isn't talking about the weather—it's never getting past it. Winners use small talk as the launchpad to take it deeper.

Here's the move: **go vertical**.

Most people stay safely neutral with horizontal, surface-level facts, polite nods, and forgettable fluff. Vertical questions shift the conversation from head to heart. That's what sticks because it speaks to something people are hungry to feel.

Just don't be weird about it.

Let's say they tell you they loved the food on their vacation. Don't stop there. Take it vertical: "What's a moment from that trip you'll never forget?" or "What surprised you most while you were there?" Engage their heart, not their personal history.

Vertical questioning is just one power tool. But if you want to keep momentum, you need more. Come prepared. Walk into the room with a few go-to, heart-level questions ready. And if nothing fits? Use the moment. Comment on the vibe, the setting, the energy—anything that naturally reopens a door.

Preparation is Everything

Load Your Arsenal Now: Craft your personal list of 3 to 5 go-to questions or topics. Keep them sharp. Use them anywhere. Make every moment count.

As you sharpen your vertical questioning, don't forget this next move. Ask questions that spark joy. When people talk about what they love, their whole energy shifts. They light up. Their guard drops.

Instead of asking, "How's work?" go with, "What's something you're really excited about right now?" or "What's the most fun thing you've done lately?" That one pivot snaps them out of autopilot and into something real.

Want to be unforgettable? Bring stories. Stories are how humans connect—always have been. You don't need to be a master storyteller. Just have two or three ready to go. Quick, real, and personal. The time you missed your flight and made a friend at the gate. That random conversation that shifted your perspective. Keep it tight. Keep it true. And when you finish? Hand the mic over. "Anything like that ever happened to you?" That's how you build momentum.

Still not clicking? Find common ground. It's the fastest way to drop the tension and get things flowing. If you realize you're not into the same things, flip it: "I've never really been into that, but a lot of people are. What got you into it?"

You're not just filling silence—you're giving them the floor. People love to teach when someone is genuinely curious.

Here's the non-negotiable: none of this works if you're faking it. People can feel forced energy from a mile away.

If you want the conversation to matter, show up honestly. Own your perspective. Be curious. Be open. That's how real connection happens. It might feel vulnerable. Good. That's the doorway.

Because small talk isn't filler; it's the bridge to something better. Every time you make someone feel welcomed into closeness, the bridge strengthens. Every time you push past the script, the connection deepens.

And if you want to get better? Don't wait. Practice. Strike up more conversations. Test what works. Watch what lands. Adjust. Improve. Confidence in conversation doesn't come from overthinking. It comes from doing.

Get Comfortable with the Pause

Let's talk about something that freaks people out—silence. A pause in conversation can feel like a gaping void you have to fill. But hold on. Silence isn't a problem. It's a power move. Let it breathe. It gives space for reflection. For someone else to jump in. For a thought to land.

If the silence stretches too long? No big deal. A simple "Look at us nailing this awkward silence. Teamwork!" resets the vibe. Humor loosens the grip. Confidence holds it steady.

See the Soul, Not the Surface

A real compliment is a spark. You don't need a dozen—just one that lands. People don't want flattery, but they want to feel understood. Skip the surface stuff like "Nice jacket." Give the kind that sinks into the soul. "The way you handled that meeting? You've got a serious talent for rallying people." Say something that speaks to who they are, not just what they show the world. Compliments like that build trust fast.

Steer Clear of Landmines

Looking to keep the flow alive? Don't spark a war. Controversial topics—politics, religion, money—can hijack a moment fast. Unless you know it's safe ground, skip the hot takes. Read the room. Redirect if things start tipping sideways.

Use Humor, Not a Hammer

Humor builds bridges if it's done right. But if you're not sure whether it's going to hit or offend? Don't say it. There are a thousand ways to be funny without offending. Smart humor adds. Thoughtless humor undercuts. Know the line. Or learn it the hard way.

Drop the Judgments

Quickest way to kill a connection? Judge. If you're sizing someone up, they'll feel it. And they'll shut down. Stop scanning for what's off and start tuning in to what's interesting. Curiosity connects. Criticism kills.

Keep It 50/50

Conversation isn't a lecture. It's a volley. Ask. Share. Respond. If you ask ten questions but offer nothing of yourself, it feels like an interrogation. But if you hog the mic, they'll tune out. It's a back-and-forth game. So rally.

Lose the Phone

Nothing murders a moment faster than glancing at your screen mid-sentence. You don't need to say, "I don't care." Your phone already said it. Real attention is rare. Be the one who gives it. If you're here, be here. Eyes up. Attention on the person in front of you. That's how connection lives.

Cut the Gossip

Talking about people behind their backs might make for juicy conversation, but it poisons trust. If you do it about others, you'll do it about me. So don't. Want to be respected? Talk about your own ideas, passions, stories—*not people.*

Know When to End It

Even great conversations have an expiration point. Are they checking their watch or scanning the room? Wrap it. Say thanks. Leave on a high note. If you really want to leave an impact, flash a genuine smile as you walk away. Your exit matters as much as your entrance. We will discuss more on ending well in future chapters.

Final Word

Perfect words won't save a conversation. But presence will. Curiosity will. The courage to be real will. People will remember how you made them feel. That's your edge. Use it, and you'll never struggle to connect again.

My Listening Breakthrough

As I first waded into the world of conversation, I used to feel like I was fumbling through every turn. Awkward pauses. Shallow small talk. Zero real connection.

One time, at a gathering, I made the ultimate rookie mistake—I asked the same question twice. Not because I didn't care but because I was so busy thinking about what to say next. I hadn't actually listened the first time.

The other person hesitated. Gave me a weird look. Walked away. Just like that, the conversation flatlined.

I beat myself up for days. Replayed the moment like a bad movie I couldn't shut off.

But here's the pivot—I didn't let that moment define me. Instead of deciding I was awkward and just "bad at conversation," I took it as a wake-up call.

I stopped trying to sound smart. Stopped trying to impress. And I started listening like it mattered.

That one shift changed everything.

Conversations got easier. People began to open up. And they didn't just talk. They engaged.

I stopped crowding the moment with noise. I made room for something honest to take root.

Fast forward to another event, and I found myself in a conversation that led to a massive opportunity. As I listened intently, the other person poured their heart out to me, and later we became close friends.

The old me would've missed it. Too distracted. Too focused on myself. But this time? I was locked in.

That's when it clicked. You don't become magnetic by saying more—but by listening better.

That's not just how you change a conversation. That's how you change your life.

Ask. Listen. Respond from the heart.

If you thought this chapter packed a punch, just wait. Because what's next isn't more of the same—it's the major leagues. Active listening is where the walls come down, and alliances are built in their place. It's the skill that shifts what people are willing to share and how deeply they trust you. You want to turn acquaintances into friends?

That's exactly where we're headed.

Stick with me.

Skies are blue. **Let's climb higher.**

***

Ending With a Bang!

You want traction? This is it. These are moves for serious momentum. Let's get rolling.

1. **Give Compliments:** Build connection fast. Offer real praise—specific, earned, from the heart. This week, hit three people with a compliment that actually means something.

2. **Practice Intently:** Carve out time every day. Talk to someone. Anyone. Practice asking deeper, listening harder, and showing up fully. That's how confidence is built—rep by rep.

3. **Respond Thoughtfully:** Every conversation is a chance to be thoughtful. Before jumping in with your take, pause. Reflect. Respond to what they just said. Do this all week. Watch what happens.

You've got the tools. Now, it's time to use them. No waiting. No rehearsing. Compliment someone today. Ask a question that gets past the surface. And for once, don't just listen—hear them.

Chapter 4 Recap: From Small Talk to Soul Talk

- **True communication isn't just about talking;** it's about making the other person feel heard and valued, transforming mere exchanges into meaningful interactions.

- **Conversations should go beyond the surface**, using open questions and inclusive tactics to invite others and create an open environment.

- **Active listening with genuine engagement is crucial**—it involves responding thoughtfully and sharing personal insights, making interactions memorable and impactful.

- **Developing conversation skills is a practice, not a talent.** It requires deliberate effort and repetition to turn small talk into valuable conversations.

Takeaway:

Talking is easy. Connecting is art. When you master presence, great questions, and real follow-through, you don't just talk—you hold the elevator for others. You ease the pressure. You say, "Come on in. Let's go up together."

May I Ask A Favor?

Hey there, Awesome Reader!

You've stumbled upon the middle of this book and haven't thrown it out the window. Congratulations! May I ask a tiny favor? Would you please pop over to the link below and write a review? Think of it as Yelp, but instead of reviewing a pizza place, you're helping the underappreciated world of words!

I know what you're thinking: "But I'm not a writer." Don't worry, neither am I! Just kidding, but seriously, it only takes a sentence or two. Something like, "This book is helpful because..." or "Five stars because this author gets me. I recommend."

Your review not only boosts my book's performance but also helps me prove to my relatives that I have a real job. Plus, every time you write a review, a writer gets their wings! (Not really, but one can dream, right?)

Who knows? Your words could be the reason someone picks up this book and finds the help they desperately need.

Thanks a million, and if you ever see me in public, pretend this never happened.

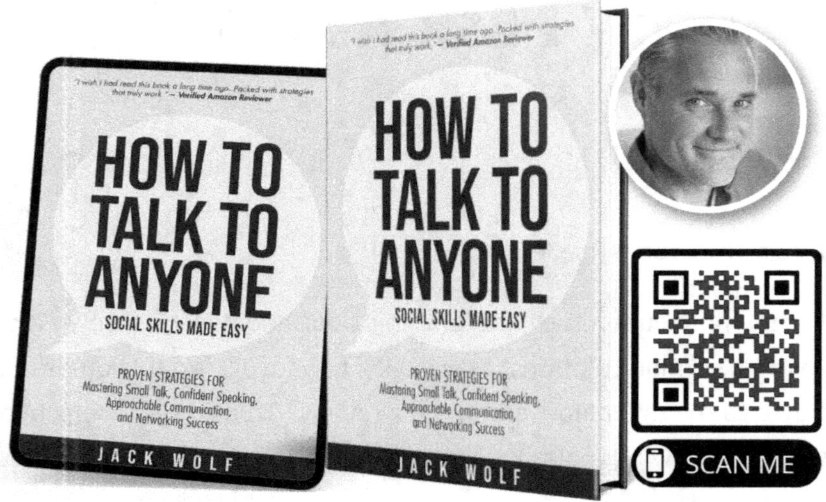

Link to Review:

https://posg.life/ReviewTalkToAnyone

Now back to the book. Keep reading!

Jack

Chapter 5

Active Listening—Or Bust

Let's cut the crap—most people think they're great listeners. They're not.

They're just waiting to talk. Nodding on autopilot. Firing up their next point before yours even lands. And when you're on the other side of that? You feel it. You feel dismissed. Unseen. Like you might as well be talking to a wall that occasionally says "uh-huh."

Here's the truth: conversation isn't connection unless someone's really listening.

And this—right here—is where most people drop the ball.

In Chapter 4, we cracked open the power of starting real conversations. But if you want those moments to go deeper, stick longer, and actually build something meaningful? You've got to learn how to truly listen like a trusted friend.

This chapter isn't about being polite. It's about mastering the one skill that flips you from surface-level to unforgettable.

It's called active listening, and once you get it, people don't just talk to you. They trust you.

What Is Active Listening—and Why Should You Care?

Active listening is more than asking vertical questions. It's full-body, full-brain, full-heart engagement. When you're actively listening, you're locked in. You're not just hearing someone's words—you're absorbing their message, their emotion, their intent. You're reading their tone, watching their body language, tuning into what's really being said—even when it's unspoken.

And here's why this matters: **people don't trust those who don't listen.**

They don't open up. They don't connect. They don't follow your lead, and they sure as heck don't build relationships that last.

The Cleveland Clinic puts it like this: "Teachers, therapists, and barbers need to be able to engage with and really hear other people all day, every day." But let's be real—we all do. Whether you're building a business, raising a family, leading a team, or just trying to connect with another human being, your ability to actively listen will determine the depth and quality of every relationship in your life.

I used to suck at listening—and it almost cost me everything.

In my marriage, I thought being a good partner meant having the right answers. Advice. Solutions. Loud opinions. What I didn't have? A clue.

We were hanging by a thread when we finally sat down with a counselor. I was sure I just needed to explain myself better. But the truth hit like a freight train: I wasn't listening. I was waiting to lead the discussion.

Then came the active listening practice sessions. They felt like mental surgery. Every instinct screamed to defend myself, argue, and win. Instead, I had to sit there, absorb her words, reflect them back—and hardest of all—stay quiet.

It felt weak. It felt slow. It felt demeaning.

But it saved us.

I learned that connection isn't about being heard. It's about making someone feel seen. And every conversation since then? It's a battle against the old instinct to bulldoze.

Sometimes I still screw it up. I don't make excuses. I reset. I refocus. I own it.

If active listening feels impossible right now? Good. It should. Struggle through it. Master it. Many people will never put in the effort to learn the skill. And that makes you incredibly special.

Real connection isn't built on how well you talk. It's built on how deeply you listen.

So, let's break down what this superpower actually gives you:

It enhances empathy. You don't just understand someone's words; you feel their perspective. You get where they're coming from, and that shifts the entire dynamic.

It builds trust. Especially in situations with uneven power dynamics. When people feel truly heard—by a boss, a partner, a parent—they start to move closer instead of pulling away.

It shows deep respect. When you hold space for someone's thoughts without interrupting or judging, you give them a rare gift: validation. That boosts confidence. That builds bonds.

It defuses conflict. Have you ever watched someone de-escalate an argument just by listening? No defensive jabs, no shouting match—just listening? That's not weakness. That's strength. It's how you take the heat out of a conversation and open a path forward.

What It Really Takes to Listen

Listening sounds simple. But doing it right? That takes incredible effort. Because real listening isn't passive. It takes all your focus.

It requires presence. Attention. Discipline.

Active listening is full-body engagement that can be felt—not just heard.

Active listening isn't about being perfect. And there are specific, concrete, doable, powerful things you can start doing today to make your listening land. Here's a high-level example of how you really listen like it matters:

First, shut up and take it in. Focus on their message—what they're saying, what they're feeling, what they're really trying to tell you. What is being said by their body, face, and tone, along with their words?

Her: "There's so much going on lately. I'm drowning in responsibilities, and housework is slipping. I need help."

Second, play it back. Reflect it back to them in your own words. Not like a robot—like a human who actually cares. Don't get defensive or try to solve.

You: "I hear that you're frustrated and want more help from me around the house."

Let them tweak it if you didn't quite catch the heart of it.

Her: "No, that's not it. I'm tired and can't keep up with housework. I want to talk about creative ways we could get it done."

Third, ask the golden question: "Is there more you want to say?" That one move opens the door wide for honesty, clarity, and trust.

Her: "Yes, you do so much for our family. I'm not necessarily asking you to take on more. I appreciate all you do."

Fourth—if there's more, loop it back to step one. You're not here to hijack the conversation. You're here to make space. Hold your take until they tell you they're done.

You: "I feel appreciated and hear you saying you aren't just loading me with more responsibility. You want to find another way."

Fifth, once she's said her piece—and you've really listened—it's your turn. Now, the door's open for real problem-solving. Maybe that means hiring a maid. Maybe it means handing the kids some extra chores. Whatever you suggest, stay open. You're not done listening just because it's your turn to talk.

That's how connection's built. One patient, powerful moment at a time. You just saw the full picture, a real moment, real emotions, real presence. Now, we're going to zoom in. Not to repeat it but to unpack it. This is where we break it down and make every moving part count.

Body language. Your body language speaks louder than your voice ever could—lean in, nod when it matters, smile because you mean it. You're not a statue—you're a live wire of attention. Your posture tells them, I'm right here with you. And they'll believe it before you ever say a word.

Eye contact is your power tool—but don't overuse it like a spotlight in someone's face. Aim for that sweet spot. The 50/70 rule is solid: make eye contact 50 to 70 percent of the time, holding it for four to five seconds before briefly looking away. Too little, and you seem disinterested. Too much, and you look like you're trying to peer into their soul. Be intentional. Be human.

Open-ended questions. Let's revisit something you nailed back in Chapter 4. They're not just great conversation starters—they're critical for listening well. Remember to ask questions that invite someone to open up, to expand, to share more than just a surface answer. Because if you're really listening, you're not just trying to get information. You're trying to understand their position and experience.

Reflection. Sure, you can say "Really?" to keep things flowing—but active listening goes deeper. That's when you start paraphrasing. Not like a parrot—but like someone who actually cares. "It sounds like you're saying…" or "Let me make sure I've got this right…" That kind of reflection shows people they're not just being heard; they're being received. It encourages them to clarify or expand, which leads to better communication all around.

Be patient. And for the love of growth, let them finish. Don't interrupt. Don't rush in with your fix or your story. Just hold the space. Let the silence stretch a little if it needs to. Most people bulldoze over silence because they're uncomfortable with it. Don't. Let the pause breathe. That pause is where clarity is born.

Drop the judgment. You want to be the person people trust with the real stuff? Then you've got to shut down the inner critic. No fixing. No correcting. No subtle face contortions that signal you think they're off base. Suspend your evaluation and meet them where they are. That creates safety, and safety creates connection.

And here's the truth: every one of these elements is a skill you can train. Not one of them is reserved for "naturally good communicators."

You don't need to be perfect. You just need to be intentional.

Take Action!

The Eye Contact Challenge: In your next three conversations, do this:

1. Put your phone away.

2. Make eye contact 50–70% of the time.

3. Hold it for 4–5 seconds before naturally breaking.

Notice how it shifts the energy. Feel the tension? Good. That means you're building muscle. And when you want to look away out of habit—don't. Stay with it. Stay with *them* because presence is power.

What Active Listening Actually Looks Like

Alright, we walked through the mechanics. You've got the tools. But now it's time to see it all come together in action. Because reading about active listening is one thing. Watching it play out in a real conversation? That's where the rubber meets the road.

Check this out. Two people. One tough night. One solid listener. Here's what it looks like when someone really shows up:

Colleen: "You won't believe the night I just had—a total blowout with my sister. Now she's not talking to me, and I feel so pissed off and just…lost."

Tony: "Wow, that sounds heavy. I'm here. What happened?"

Simple. Direct. No fixing. Just an open door.

Colleen: "It started over something stupid. Our parents' anniversary party. She wants this huge, expensive thing. I told her I couldn't afford it. She wouldn't even try to understand where I was coming from."

Tony: "Sounds like you felt completely shut out like your side didn't even matter."

Boom. That's not just "I hear you"—that's "I feel you." That's reflection with presence.

Colleen: "Exactly! And now, I feel guilty because I love my parents and want to do something nice, but I don't want to pretend I can give what I can't. I told her to do it without me, but that feels awful too."

Tony: "Yeah, no wonder you're torn. You're stuck between guilt, pressure, and wanting to be heard. That's a lot to hold. Is there more?"

No advice. No quick fixes. Only validation and empathy. Judgment stays out of it.

Colleen: "No. Thank you. Seriously. I just needed someone to listen."

That's it. That's the win. She didn't need a savior. She didn't need a solution. She needed to feel seen. And Tony—just by being present, reflecting back what he heard, and letting her lead—gave her exactly that.

That's the power of active listening. It's not magic. It's presence. It's patience. And when you show up like that, people don't just feel heard. They feel safe.

Benefits of Active Listening in Different Relationships

Fact: If you want better relationships, you've got to get out of your own head and into the world of the person in front of you. Active listening isn't just a technique; it's a relationship game-changer. So, where does this superpower pay off? Everywhere. But let's get specific. Because the way you listen to your boss isn't the way you listen to your partner.

Personal Relationships

In your close relationships—friends, family, the people who matter most—active listening sends a clear message: you're safe with me. When someone feels safe to share their thoughts without judgment, they open up. That builds intimacy. It strengthens bonds.

It tells your people, "I'm not just here to hear you. I'm here to understand you." And that's rare. That's powerful. That's what makes you the person they come back to when things get real.

Romantic Relationships

Let's talk love. Real love—the kind that lasts—demands more than chemistry. It demands clarity, communication, and trust. And nothing builds that faster than active listening. When you actually hear your partner without jumping in, cutting them off, or trying to fix everything, you prove you value them. You stop the assumptions, reduce the fights, and create space for vulnerability. That's how two people grow deeper, not apart.

Professional Relationships

Think this skill is just for your closest people? Think again. In the workplace, it's a secret weapon. Listening well makes you a better teammate, a better leader, and a better human to work with. It shows respect. It cuts through confusion. It turns colleagues into collaborators and transforms meetings from "talking at" to "working with." If you want to earn trust at work, don't try to sound smart. Listen smart.

New Relationships

And what about the new connections—the fresh faces, the potential allies, partners, or friends? This is where active listening lays the foundation. First impressions are everything, and when you show someone they're not just being heard but understood? You fast-track trust. You skip the surface and get to real rapport. From day one, you become the kind of person people want in their corner.

Reframe Your Fear: People Need You

Most people go their whole lives without feeling truly heard. Be the exception. Be the one who listens so well that others feel lighter just being around you.

When someone opens up, don't flinch. Take a breath. Lock in. Your ability to listen isn't just helpful. It's healing. It calms storms. It opens doors. It makes you magnetic.

You want real influence? Build it one moment of presence at a time. Not by saying more but by proving you've already heard what matters.

And yeah—because it's like a muscle, you strengthen it by doing. Every conversation is a rep. A chance to either build connection or skip leg day. Your choice.

If you want to go from decent to dangerous in this skill, here's the move: listen with intention. Reflect what you hear. Stay in the moment. Stay in your lane. Validate instead of fixing. Circle back. That's how trust gets built.

Active listening isn't soft. It's sharp. It's power with precision. And when you use it like this? You don't just become someone people hear. You become someone they feel.

You've unlocked one of the most overlooked tools in human connection. Now, let's add fuel to the fire.

Because the words you speak? They're only half the story.

Next up: the signals you don't even realize you're sending. Body language. Tone. Presence. If you want to read people like a book—and write a better one while you're at it—don't miss what's coming.

Let's turn the volume up on everything you don't say.

***

Ending With a Bang!

Want to turn active listening into a real-world superpower? Good—let's get to work.

1. **Make Active Listening a Non-Negotiable.** For the next seven days, keep track of your daily conversations. Jot down the moments where you were fully dialed in—fully present, fully listening—and the times you slipped into distraction, interruption, or autopilot. What pulled you in? What pulled you out? Awareness gives you power to improve.

2. **Reflect and Paraphrase Like a Pro.** Grab a friend or colleague and run this drill: One person talks for a solid minute—any topic. The other listens, then paraphrases what they heard. Switch roles. Do this a few rounds. You'll be shocked at how much your brain wants to drift. But if you can stay present here, you'll stay present anywhere.

3. **Validate Without Jumping In.** The next time a friend opens up, resist the urge to fix it or give advice. Just listen—and validate. Say things like, "That makes total sense," or "I'd feel the same way in your shoes." Let them sit with their thoughts. You don't need to fix it to be in their corner. Just remind them they're not alone.

4. **Learn From Every Interaction.** At the end of each day, take five minutes and reflect. Think about one or two conversations you had. Where did you show up well and where did you check out? Keep a running journal. Over time, this will reveal patterns. As you see the patterns, you can address them.

Chapter 5 Recap: Active Listening—Or Bust

- **Hearing isn't listening.** Dive deep into the real conversation, where you feel every word, see every emotion, and truly connect.

- **Master active listening** to unlock empathy, build trust, and forge lasting connections. It's about engaging with the heart, not just the ears.

- **Stay fully present.** Lock in with eye contact, tune into the tone, and lean in to show you're right there with them.

- **Use open-ended questions** to open up real dialogue. Make each question a bridge to deeper understanding.

- **Be genuine. Reflect and validate your partner.** Transform every chat into a meaningful connection without rushing to respond.

Takeaway:

Active listening is your secret weapon. It's more than hearing—it's understanding and connecting on a deeper level. Kickstart your journey to becoming a communication powerhouse by truly listening, engaging deeply, and making every conversation count. Get into it now, and watch your relationships transform.

Chapter 6

Talking Without Your Words

She was a brick wall.

I said all the right words. Stayed on topic. Made my point. Still... nothing landed.

What the heck just happened?

Real communication isn't just about what you say—it's about how you say it and what your body's saying when your mouth isn't yapping.

Words are just the tip of the iceberg. The real magic—or the real mess—happens in the silent signals: your body language, tone, facial expressions, and gestures. These signals are powerful. They can pull people in, create trust, and deepen connection. Or they can quietly sabotage your message, even if your intentions are golden.

Take it from Ruth H. Nobile, a chemist at Bayer Pharmaceuticals and a professor at Rutgers. She wrote about leading her first team meeting. She spent hours studying, rehearsing, getting ready to crush it. But the moment she stepped in front of the room, her confidence cracked—shoulders slumped, smile disappeared. Her tone went flat. And just like that, she started losing the room.

Her words hadn't changed, but her presence had. Her nonverbal cues started screaming insecurity, and the team felt it. But here's what made the difference: she noticed. She recalibrated—stood tall, smiled, focused. And by the end of that meeting, she had them back in her corner. Why? Because her body finally matched the confidence she'd worked so hard to build.

That's what this chapter is about—taking control of the part of your communication that most people never even think about. You're going to learn how to read others without a single word being said. You're going to master the signals your face, hands, body, and tone are already sending and start using them with precision.

When you do, you won't just talk to people. You'll connect. You'll lead. You'll become unforgettable.

Let's break it down.

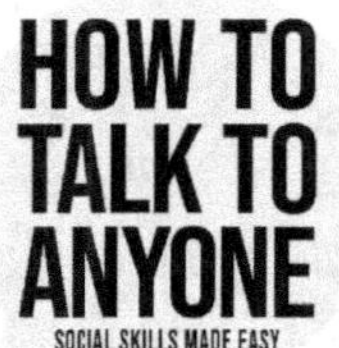

… Written by a natural wallflower who still throws up in his mouth a little at big gatherings, yet he knows how to gain influence and make friends.

What Is Nonverbal Communication?

Wrap your brain around this reality—**your mouth isn't doing most of the talking.**

You might think your words carry the weight. But science says otherwise: **80% of what you communicate is nonverbal** (VeryWell Mind, 2024). That's right—your face, your tone, your posture, your gestures—they're all talking before you ever open your mouth.

Maybe the better title for this book would've been **How to Talk to Anyone Without Talking**.

Nonverbal communication is how your body fills in the blanks, backs up your words, or combats them directly. Strong eye contact and posture shape how you're read—fast. We'll break down exactly how to master them later.

Let's define the large groupings in this silent symphony:

Facial Expressions

Your face is a flashing billboard for your emotions. Joy, rage, guilt, boredom. You don't even have to say a word. And then there are microexpressions. Those blink-and-you'll-miss-it flashes that leak the truth, even when your mouth is trying to hide it. If your words say, "I'm fine," but your face says, "I'm two seconds from losing it," guess which one people believe?

Gestures

Your hands aren't just there to hold coffee. They clarify, emphasize, or sometimes replace your words entirely. A nod can mean agreement. A wave can say goodbye. A thumbs-up can seal a deal. Or blow the deal if used at the wrong time.

Paralinguistics (tone of voice)

Tone, speed, pitch—this is the emotional layer under your words. Speak too fast, and you sound panicked; too slow, and you seem unsure—or worse, boring. Tone flips the meaning behind your words. We'll break it down fully later.

Body Language and Posture

Your posture screams before your voice does. Lean in, and you say, "I'm with you." Fold your arms and lean back, and you say, "I'm done here." Most of us don't even realize the messages we're sending with our bodies, but others do.

Road hazard ahead! Nonverbal communication doesn't just support your words—it can override them. You might say all the right things, but if your face, your body, or your tone says otherwise, that's what people are going to believe.

Think about the last time you met someone new. Maybe it was at a party, on a date, or during your kid's soccer game. If you were fidgeting, crossing your arms, or looking away, they didn't hear your words. They felt your energy. And they probably walked away thinking you weren't interested.

But if you were smiling, making solid eye contact, leaning in when they spoke? You didn't just seem friendly. You felt magnetic.

This is the power of nonverbal communication. It can build trust faster than words ever will. It can show warmth, confidence, curiosity, or shut people down in a second. It deepens relationships, signals attraction, regulates the flow of a conversation, and sometimes... it says the things we don't know how—or aren't ready—to say out loud.

Mastering it means unlocking a new level of connection, whether you're in the boardroom, the bar, or your living room. Let's sharpen that skill next.

Decoding Facial Expressions

Don't kid yourself—your face snitches on you. You aren't as in control as you may think.

Emotions don't always match the script, and your face is usually the first place the truth shows up. You can dress up your words, put on a calm voice, rehearse a script all day long—but your face? Busted.

Facial expressions are the first giveaway in any interaction. And if you're not reading them right—or worse, not controlling your own—you're playing social poker with your cards face-up *(VeryWell Mind*, 2024).

Here's a wild example: duping delight. It's when someone lies and their face, specifically their mouth, gives them away. They might smirk, just for a flash, because their brain is secretly thrilled it's getting away with something. That flicker? That's the moment the mask slips. And if you're paying attention, you'll catch it.

Now, facial expressions can vary a bit across cultures, but some are basically universal—anger, sadness, joy, fear, disgust, surprise. These show up everywhere, from New York to Nairobi. The catch? We're best at reading people from our own culture. *Psychology Today* (2016) backs this up: we naturally "read" those who were raised the same way we were. So, if you're talking to someone from a different cultural background, slow down. Skip the sarcasm. Clarify when needed. Smile like a human, not like a smirking emoji.

Here's a personal story:

A friend of mine—16, wide-eyed, just landed in Paris. He was delighted to be immersed in the culture, spending the whole trip smiling and locking eyes with strangers. Totally innocent. Totally unaware. And totally shocked by how many French locals read that as: "Hey, I'm interested... romantically." Moral of the story? Your face can flirt without your permission. Know what you're saying, especially when you're not talking.

Understanding Body Language and Gestures

Your face starts the conversation. Your body finishes it.

In fact, your body reveals what your mouth keeps hidden. *PsychCentral* (2021) says it best: "At the most basic level, body language is an external signal of a person's inner emotional state. Body language is the story our bodies tell about how we think and feel."

Some of it's obvious. A stomped foot? Angry. A thumbs up? Nailed it. But not all signals are that clean. A shift in weight, a twitch of the arm, a slight lean away—those whispers matter.

If you're only listening to words, you're reading half the story. But when you start tracking body language, you level up. You start spotting unspoken emotion, unsaid tension, hidden hesitations—and that makes you a sharper communicator, a better friend, a stronger leader.

Here's one you already know but may not have mastered yet: eye contact.

Nail it, and you're magnetic. Avoid it, and you look shady—or scared. In the early stages of any relationship, eye contact is what builds trust. In close relationships, it deepens connection. And in any setting? It shows you're present, not halfway out the mental door.

Now, add posture to the mix. You slouch, you shrink. You stand tall, you signal confidence—even if your knees are shaking. Want to be taken seriously? Roll your shoulders back, lift your chin, and act like you belong in the room.

And don't underestimate this—people notice. Whether you're pitching an idea, introducing yourself at a party, or just ordering coffee, your body is telling others whether or not they should be interested. Make sure it's in agreement with your intentions.

In a moment, we'll break down the rest of the body language playbook, but before we do, here's the takeaway:

You already speak nonverbally. You just didn't know the vocabulary.

Now, let's make it fluent.

Take Action!

Mirror a Conversation Partner: Pair up with a partner and engage in a conversation. Deliberately mirror your partner's body language, then switch roles. Afterward, discuss how mirroring affected your feelings of connection and understanding.

How to Read Body Language

While words can be deceptive and gestures misleading, your overall body language paints a clearer picture. Get it wrong, and you'll leave others with unease and suspicion.

Let's start with the face. A real smile doesn't just stretch across your lips—it lights up your eyes too. Look for the tiny crinkles at the corners. No crinkles, no real smile. If the smile is tight and flat, and the eyes stay frozen? Fake. No matter how wide their mouth goes, if their eyes aren't playing along, they're not feeling it. And if they're smiling at you with locked-in eye contact that lasts longer than casual? Newsflash—they might be into you.

Continue watching the **eyes**. Blink patterns are a dead giveaway. Rapid blinking usually signals nerves or stress. Dilated pupils, though? Excitement, interest, attraction—they're loving what they see. Direct eye contact shows engagement. But stare too long without a break, and you'll come off as aggressive or creepy. Eye blocking (covering the eyes or looking away) screams discomfort or straight-up deception. People instinctively shield their eyes when they're feeling off.

Arms and legs tell another story. Crossed arms or legs? Defensive. Resistant. Closed for business. Open, relaxed arms? They're welcoming you in. As we've covered earlier, people who shove an arm behind their back or clutch something to their chest aren't relaxed—they're throwing up invisible shields.

Feet spill even more secrets. They're brutally honest. If someone's toes are pointed toward you, they're locked in. If their feet start drifting toward the door, believe them. Their mind has already left the conversation.

Hands! Clenched fists, tight fingers, white-knuckled grips—all of them shout tension, anger, or frustration. Open palms, on the other hand, scream honesty, openness, and a non-threatening vibe. And if someone's hand drifts up to touch their cheek while you're talking? You've got their attention. They're thinking carefully or showing genuine interest. If they scratch their nose, they're probably lying to you.

Personal space matters, too. Standing close usually shows comfort—or intimacy if it's the right context. But without checking other cues, it can also feel aggressive. Distance, meanwhile, can mean discomfort or disengagement. Different cultures have different rules for space, so read the room. What's friendly in one place can be deeply offensive in another. If you're dealing with someone from a different culture, don't guess—learn what signals are respectful and what signals could accidentally pick a fight.

There's another level to this: how much space you own. Someone who sits tall, legs apart, arms spread naturally? They're showing confidence and authority without saying a word. Small, tight, hunched-up postures communicate the opposite: insecurity, anxiety, fear. Used right, big gestures show power. Used wrong, and you'll look like you're conducting an invisible orchestra.

One more thing most people miss: **neurodiversity and psychological differences** change the whole game. *Healthline* (2020) points out, "Neurodiverse people may also use and interpret body language differently than neurotypical people do." Someone who's neurodiverse might not catch that you're trying to wrap up the conversation—or they might not realize their body language is sending different signals. Same with psychological differences. You've got to stay sharp, patient, and empathetic. Not everybody plays by the same nonverbal rules, and that's not a license to judge.

Mastering body language is about awareness, not mind-reading. Stack little clues until they paint a bigger picture. The more you watch, the more obvious it gets. And the better you get, the easier it becomes to connect, influence, and lead.

Take Action!

Posture Awareness Exercise: Start right now with this killer move: Set a random alarm during your day. When it buzzes, don't just check your phone—check yourself. What's your posture like? Are you slouching, closing up, shrinking? Fix it. Stand tall. Breathe deep. Own the space you're in. You'll feel the shift, and so will everyone around you.

Analyzing Tone

You've heard it before: It's not what you say—it's how you say it. And guess what? It's absolutely true. Your tone can either hype up your words or betray you, ruining the whole conversation.

Tone is one of the sneakiest, most powerful parts of nonverbal communication. It's not just about volume—it's your pace, your pitch, your rhythm. It's the emotional fingerprint behind every word you say. People don't just hear you. They feel you.

Why Tone Matters

According to *Customers First Academy* (2024), "When our tone isn't aligned with our words, it can create confusion and misinterpretation." Translation? You can say all the right words and still blow it if your tone tells a different story.

If your tone is sharp while you're saying, "I'm fine," nobody's buying it. If your voice is shaky while you're "totally confident," the whole room feels the tremble.

Quick Reality Check: What Your Tone's Telling People

A deep voice commands authority and strength.

A soft, quiet voice pulls people in and whispers trust.

A steady, confident tone lays down certainty.

Calm breathing under your words? People relax.

Rapid, shallow breaths? They pick up on your nerves whether you want them to or not.

A warm tone? That's the cheat code to instant likability.

A harsh or rushed tone? Good luck keeping people close.

How to Master Your Tone

Listen to yourself. Do you match your tone to the emotion partnered with your message? When you compliment someone, sound upbeat. Deliver hard news? Stay calm but firm. Don't just memorize the right words—make sure your voice wears them properly.

Second, stay sharp. Speak clearly. Don't mumble, don't ramble, don't over-dramatize every syllable like you're auditioning for a soap opera. When you keep your words clean and focused, you make it easy for others to follow and connect.

Last tip? Be friendly. Seriously. Warmth is a secret weapon most people are too cold or guarded to use. A likable tone builds bridges faster than a thousand clever lines ever could.

If you have the choice to sound cool or sound kind, always choose kind—you'll win people's trust without even trying.

Bottom line: Your tone is either opening doors or closing them. Train it like your social life depends on it—because it does.

From Knowing to Owning: What to Practice

You've loaded up your toolbox with the fundamentals—facial expressions, body language, gestures, and tone. Now it's time to move from knowing to doing. Mastering nonverbal communication isn't about being perfect right out of the gate. It's about getting sharper, smarter, and more connected every time you use them.

Here's how to lock it in.

Catch the Gaps

When people's words and bodies don't always sync up, that's your signal to pay attention. If someone's saying everything's "great," but their eyes are darting or their body's pulling away, don't fly past it. Notice the mismatch. Lean in gently. Ask kindly if they'd like to talk about what's really going on. Sometimes, the real conversation is happening underneath what's being said out loud.

Match Your Message

You already know your body either backs you up or blows you up. Now, practice making every signal count. Double-check that your body isn't undermining your words. Smile when you mean it. Open up your posture when you're welcoming someone in. Let people see the real you without mixed signals getting in the way. It's time to stop defending yourself at the onset of conversations.

Read the Room

Context matters. The body language you throw around with your buddies at a barbecue? Probably not going to fly at a boardroom meeting. Pay attention to the setting you're in and adjust how you present. Smart communicators flex their nonverbal cues to fit the environment without losing who they are.

Look at the Whole Picture

One offbeat moment doesn't tell the whole story. Good communicators don't zero in on one thing, like a quick glance away or a nervous fidget, and build a whole narrative around it. Step back. Watch how someone's face, voice, hands, and energy all fit together before you jump to conclusions. Patterns matter more than one-off moves.

Stay Sharp When Signals Get Scrambled

Nonverbal communication isn't a perfect science. It's an art. Sometimes, you'll misread someone, and sometimes they'll misread you. If something feels off, use your words to reset the vibe. "Hey, I'm picking up that you're a little uncomfortable—is that right?" Clear, human check-ins can fix a lot of what gets lost in translation.

Breathe Through the Nerves

If you're getting stressed, your body's going to rat you out. Tight shoulders. Shaky voice. Fidgety hands. One of the fastest ways to steady yourself is your breath. Slow it down, breathe deeply, and own the moment. Calm energy sends strong signals that you're grounded even when the pressure's on.

Use Your Hands—But Don't Let Them Run the Show

Some of us talk with our hands like we're landing planes on the runway.

(Guilty.) It's not a bad thing unless the gestures get wild enough to distract from your message. Keep your hand movements clean and intentional. If it backs up what you're saying, use it. If it's just noise, tell yourself to relax. Feel your smile through your whole body. You are enough. Let go of the pressure to impress others.

Train Like You Mean It

Nobody's born a world-class communicator. They train for it. Practice paying attention to nonverbal cues in every conversation you have. Watch. Adjust. Repeat. Over time, you'll stop overthinking it and start reading people—and yourself—naturally. Commit to learning from conversations without obsessing over mistakes. Be kind to yourself.

Level Up With Mirroring

Mirroring is the ultimate ace card. It's when you subtly match someone's body language, tone, or energy without copying them like a bad impersonation. Done right, it builds instant trust. Done wrong, it feels fake. Watch closely. Match the vibe, not the motions. If they're relaxed, you relax. If they're leaning in, you lean a little too. Let it flow instead of forcing it.

Mirroring can be verbal, too—matching someone's tone, pacing, or phrasing just enough to show you're synced. The goal isn't mimicry—it's connection. Stay real, stay aware, and you'll build bridges without anyone even realizing it.

Want to drill this in? Flip to the Appendix at the end of the book. You'll find a ready-to-roll checklist that'll keep your nonverbal game sharp and simple. Any time, any place.

What's Next: Get Ready to Play at a Higher Level

You've just cracked the code on nonverbal communication—the silent language that makes or breaks every conversation you have. You now know how to read the room and how to own the space you're in.

This wraps up **Part II.**

Next up, we're diving even deeper—into the heart of what makes deeper connection possible: empathy, emotional intelligence, and the secret ingredients that make strangers into allies.

You're not here to blend in. You're here to be felt. Heard. Remembered. Buckle up and prepare to transform.

***

Ending With a Bang!

Seize the moment. Make it stick. It's time to move from learning to living it. Take bold action with these next steps:

1. **Master the Power of Silence.** In your next conversation, hit the brakes before you respond. Let silence hang for a beat. Watch how it pulls people in and deepens the connection.

2. **Engage in People Watching.** Park yourself somewhere busy. Skip the eavesdropping. Watch body language only. Guess the story based on what you see—if possible, check if you were right.

3. **Run a Non-Verbal Audit.** In your next meeting, don't just hear the words—watch the room. Track your own non-verbal signals, too. Figure out what's building trust...and what's breaking it.

4. **Teach It Forward.** The best way to learn is to teach. Find someone who hasn't even thought about non-verbal communication. Break it down for them in real-world examples.

Chapter 6 Recap: Talking Without Your Words

- **Your mouth isn't doing most of the talking.** 80% of communication is nonverbal.

- **Your face snitches first.** Real smiles, microexpressions, cultural cues—read them or miss the truth.

- **Body language carries the conversation.** Posture, eye contact, gestures, and space say it all.

- **Tone makes or breaks your message.** Match your emotion to your words. Warmth wins.

- **Mastery isn't magic.** Stack small clues. Mirror naturally. Breathe through the nerves.

- **Connection beats perfection.** The goal isn't flawless moves—it's authentic, powerful connection.

Takeaway:

Your presence speaks before you do. Command it. Shape it. Walk into every room like you're already the one people want to follow.

Part III

Speak Boldly. Live Bigger.

Chapters 7 – 9

"The two words 'information' and 'communication' are often used interchangeably, but they signify quite different things. Information is giving out; communication is getting through." **—Sydney J. Harris**

Most people live muted lives: talking without impact, connecting without depth, settling without even realizing it. But not you. You're here to rip the mask off, step into the mess, and make conversations matter.

No more playing small. No more polite invisibility.

In these chapters, you'll master the real weapons of connection: empathy that offends the inauthentic, boundaries fierce enough to carve your space, trust that sticks because it's earned, and boldness that kicks doors clean off their hinges.

This isn't about getting noticed. It's about being unforgettable.

By the time you're done here, you won't just walk into rooms—you'll reshape them. You'll speak with fire, live with guts, and leave every encounter stronger than you found it.

Speak boldly. Live bigger. Leave a mark they can't erase.

Chapter 7

Empathy: Step into the Mess

"If you say uh-huh one more time, I'm going to go ballistic!"

Ever felt like you're pouring your heart out, but it's just vanishing into the void? That's because, without empathy, even the loudest shout is just a whisper in the wind.

Let's cut to the chase: If people can't feel your heartbeat in your words, they'll never truly hear what you're saying. Even with the polish of an Oscar winner, without real connection, it's all just an act. And real life isn't a scripted show—it's raw, it's real, and it demands real empathy.

Imagine Elena Aguilar's battlefield: a classroom where her struggle as a teacher transformed into an epic breakthrough in empathy. She cared for a student, "T," who distanced herself through silence and defiance. Weeks of frustration and failed attempts had built walls too high to peer over. Then, a simple classroom exercise accidentally cracked everything wide open. Elena asked her students, "If you could have one wish, what would it be?" While others wished for fame or fortune, "T" wished for something startlingly simple yet profound: new clothes because hers were secondhand and worn.

This revelation shattered Elena's preconceptions like glass under a hammer, clearing the dense fog of misunderstanding clouding their interactions. At that moment, when "T" expressed her simple yet profound wish, a bridge was built. Elena no longer saw a defiant student across the chasm of disconnect; she saw a young person in need, vulnerable and sincere. This spark of deep, empathetic connection ignited a transformation in their relationship.

It was as if Elena had been dialing into a distant signal, and with empathy, the static cleared, and the message came through loud and clear. "T" felt truly seen, perhaps for the first time in that classroom, not as a problem to be solved but as a person to be valued and understood. This shift marked the beginning of a new chapter for both teacher and student—one where trust was the foundation, and genuine connection was the gradual result.

This wasn't some kind of magic. This was raw empathy in action, turning deadlock into dynamic breakthrough. This single moment of understanding shifted the dynamic of their entire relationship, proving that empathy can bridge even the widest gaps.

In this chapter, we dive deep into how empathy transforms surface-level exchanges into profound, lasting connections. Empathy is more than an open ear; it's stepping into someone's shoes, feeling with them, and seeing their world—not just hearing their words but truly understanding their heartbeat. It takes our interactions beyond the superficial and stitches the fabric of genuine relationships.

This isn't just feel-good fluff. Empathy isn't just some nice idea cooked up by self-help gurus in cozy sweaters. It's been studied. For example, researchers found that when doctors show real empathy—not just nodding along but truly connecting—patients trust them more, follow through better, and even heal faster. Yeah, you read that right.

One study published in the *British Journal of General Practice* showed that empathy wasn't just helpful—it was transformational. Patients felt more satisfied, less anxious, and way more likely to actually follow their treatment plan when they felt their doctor truly understood them (Derksen et al., 2013).

So, if empathy can do that in a doctor's office? Imagine what it can do in your conversations, your relationships, and your life.

We're not here to learn better small talk. There are other books more suited for that. We're here to build trust, connection, and understanding that actually changes people. One conversation at a time.

And here is some great news! Empathy isn't some mystical gift you're born with. It's a skill you build like a muscle. And science backs it up. Klimecki and her team showed that when people trained for empathy, their brains actually changed—and they showed up in the real world with more compassion, more action, more heart (Klimecki et al., 2014).

So, buckle up. We're moving beyond the surface chatter. It's time to explore how to wield empathy—not just as a concept but as a concrete tool that empowers us to make every human encounter richer and more meaningful.

What is Empathy Exactly?

When you tap into empathy, you're telling the other person, "I get you. You're not alone in this." It validates their feelings, which is more than reflecting back what you hear in order to better understand.

And it isn't sympathy. Sympathy stays dry on the shore, calling out encouragement. Empathy dives in, swims beside them, and feels the current. That's the difference. One comforts from a distance. The other connects at the core. By embedding ourselves in the emotional currents of others, we don't just feel sorry for others—we become an ally. Every conversation creates deeper, more meaningful connections, enriching our lives and those around us with genuine engagement.

Let's press into empathy as we aim to turn our conversations into powerful, lasting relationships!

Now, empathy might seem like a puzzle, with everyone describing different pieces based on what they've been through. It's a multi-layered beast, and each layer digs unique tunnels, enriching how we connect with folks around us. None of the following is right or wrong—or better or worse. They are simply different levels through which people may empathize with others:

- **Cognitive Empathy:** This is the ability to understand another person's perspective or mental state, which is essential for effective communication. It's about acknowledging thoughts and why someone might feel a certain way without necessarily experiencing those feelings yourself.

- **Emotional Empathy:** This is what allows us to actually feel the pain or joy of others, creating a shared emotional experience. This type of empathy can lead to profound bonds as it involves not just understanding but also feeling another's emotions.

- **Compassionate Empathy:** Going beyond understanding and feeling, this type of empathy moves us to take action to help however we can. It's empathy in action, driving us to do something to alleviate someone's distress or enhance their happiness.

When you strengthen your empathy, everything changes. You don't just improve your relationships—you become someone who makes the world feel safer, stronger, and more connected. Interactions grow from simple talks to meaningful, lasting relationships as you become an ally in other people's struggles and experiences.

Let's see how these concepts play out in everyday life, beyond theoretical discussion, where a simple outing between two of my friends illustrates the profound difference empathy can make.

Jill and Margaret: Real-World Empathy

On a brisk evening, Jill and Margaret left the comfort of a well-lit parking garage, heading toward a cozy downtown bistro they frequented. As they chatted about their week, laughter echoing between them, a figure huddled under a worn blanket on the sidewalk caught their eyes. A homeless man sat there, his gaze fixed on a small, battered cup filled with a few coins.

Margaret's expression softened immediately, and she murmured, "Oh, that poor man," digging into her purse for a dollar. She dropped the bill into his cup from a distance, offering a brief, sympathetic smile before quickly moving on. "I feel so sorry for him," she said to Jill as they continued walking, her voice tinged with sadness yet carrying a hint of distance.

Jill paused, her eyes lingering on the man. Unlike Margaret, she felt a pull to understand more and to connect on a human level that went beyond monetary assistance. With a gentle nod to Margaret, she stepped closer to the man, her approach cautious but open.

"Hi there," Jill began, her voice warm and inviting. "It looks really chilly tonight, doesn't it?"

The man looked up, seemingly surprised by the directness and warmth of her address. Encouraged by his gaze, she continued, "My friend and I are just heading to dinner. Can we get you something to eat?"

The man's eyes widened slightly, and he nodded, his voice barely above a whisper. "A coffee would be nice, thank you."

As Margaret watched, she noticed the change not just in the man's demeanor but also in Jill's. Jill wasn't just offering help; she was engaging him in a moment of shared humanity. They weren't two disparate entities divided by circumstance; for that moment, they shared the cold bite of the wind and the warmth of potential friendship.

Jill smiled and asked, "How do you take it?"

"Just black," he replied, a small smile breaking through his guarded expression.

"Coming right up," Jill said cheerfully, then turned to Margaret. "I'll catch up in a sec. Can you save us a spot?"

Margaret watched, a complex mix of emotions visible on her face as Jill entered the café. She didn't just buy a coffee; she also picked up a sandwich, ensuring the man would have something substantial to eat. Returning, Jill handed him both the coffee and the sandwich with a gentle, "Stay warm, okay?"

The man's thanks were subtle but heartfelt, a stark contrast to the brief interaction he had with Margaret. As Jill rejoined Margaret, the difference was clear. While Margaret's sympathy was fleeting, Jill's empathy created a connection, recognizing the man's humanity and engaging with it directly.

As they dined, Margaret reflected aloud, "You really made a difference, Jill. I gave money, but you gave him a moment of your time."

Jill nodded, her response simple yet deep, "Sometimes, it's not just about helping; it's about connecting. It doesn't take much, but it can change someone's night—or even their life."

See the difference? Margaret stood on the shore. Jill dove in. Sympathy steps back. Empathy steps forward—and that's where real connection begins.

It's not merely recognizing that someone is experiencing a particular moment; it's about understanding the depth of their emotions from their vantage point, sharing in their experience without judgment or reservation. It's about living in it for a moment, seeing through their eyes, and feeling with their heart.

This is why empathy can be so transformative—it connects, heals, and builds trust in ways that simple acknowledgment cannot achieve.

What's Blocking Your Empathy?

Let's not sugarcoat it—if empathy came easy to everyone, the world wouldn't be such a mess. But it doesn't. There are mental walls, subconscious patterns, and learned behaviors that get in the way. If you want to grow, you've got to know what's standing in your path.

First up: **cognitive bias.** This one's sneaky. It's the filter your brain uses to process the world, and it usually got installed before you were old enough to question it. Maybe you grew up hearing, "People on the street just don't want to work." That belief sinks in deep. So when you pass someone struggling, empathy doesn't even get a chance to show up—because the bias has already slammed the door shut. Sound harsh? That's the point. Bias blinds you.

Then there's **dehumanization**. It happens when you mentally file someone as "not like me." They're too different. Too far removed. And suddenly, their pain doesn't hit the same. Think about seeing a war-torn country on the news. You feel sad, maybe. But if it happened down your street? Different story, right? Dehumanization is indifference dressed up as distance—and it kills connection.

And let's talk about **victim blaming**. This one's brutal. Something bad happens to someone, and instead of empathy, we go, "Well... maybe they brought it on themselves." Why? Because it gives us a false sense of control. If we believe they deserved it, then we believe we can avoid it. But that's not empathy—it's self-preservation pretending to be justice. And it leaves people isolated when they need understanding most.

Bias blinds. Dehumanization disconnects. But empathy? It rewires how we see people. Psychologist C. Daniel Batson's research backs it—empathy doesn't just feel good; it breaks down prejudice and builds real connection (Batson et al., 1997).

And just like any skill worth building, it comes with resistance. But now that you know an obstacle in the way? You've got no excuse to stay stuck.

Time to Take the Wheel!

Reflect on Your Experiences: Think of a moment when someone really showed up for you. No judgment. No fixing. Just honest, raw empathy. Write it down. What did they do? How did it shift you? That memory is your blueprint.

Practical Steps to Develop Empathy

Empathy might not be your first language, but you can learn to speak it fluently. All it takes is practice, grit, and being available. And these days? It matters more than ever. We're drowning in noise but starving for real connection. People don't need more clever words—they need to be felt, understood, and seen. That's where you come in.

While mastering empathy might seem like a tall order—and yes, it's a bit more than we can cover in just one book—you can kickstart your journey right here. Start practicing the following core empathy skills in this section. Seek out people in your life who seem to display an understanding of empathy and get into conversations with them. Want to dive deeper or hit me up directly? Swing by my contact page at https://posg.life/contact. Let's make this world a little less lonely together.

Now, to begin to develop empathy, start with **being present**. In today's world, it's easy to get distracted. But being present means more than just physically being there. It involves engaging fully with the person you're with. Whether it's a casual chat or a deep conversation, stay in the moment, free from distractions. This shows that you value the interaction and are genuinely interested in understanding their experience.

Next is an important skill we learned: **active listening**. This means you listen to understand, not just to respond. By focusing on not only the words they use but the tone of their voice and the emotions they are expressing, we absorb the feelings behind them. And that's key to empathy. If you can't observe someone else's feelings, you won't be able to ultimately validate them.

Asking open questions is another tool in building empathy. Instead of questions that lead to a simple yes or no, encourage others to open up more. Ask how a particular event made them feel or what it meant to them. This not only deepens the conversation but also shows that you care about their deeper thoughts and emotions.

Finally, practice **empathetic validation**. This means recognizing and acknowledging someone's feelings without judgment. Expressions like, "This must feel so conflicting for you," or "I can see why you'd feel that way," can go a long way. Even if you don't fully agree with their perspective, you can validate their feelings. These phrases show that you are not just listening but also connecting with their emotional experience.

To make empathy a real game-changer in your life and transform your daily interactions, get into the habit of setting specific, actionable goals for strengthening each skill. Start with something manageable—like tuning in with active listening at least once every day or connecting with a compassionate action each week. As you get the hang of it, ramp up the frequency and challenge yourself with more complex scenarios.

Empathy in Action

Imagine a colleague is stressed about an upcoming deadline or a friend is upset over a personal issue. By applying empathy—listening actively, being fully present, asking open questions, and validating their feelings—you don't just offer comfort; you build a bridge of genuine understanding and support.

In fact, empathy isn't just a "nice-to-have" in relationships—it's a power move. People naturally see leaders in others, regardless of their role or title.

According to **Harvard Business School**, leaders who lead with empathy crush it in coaching, decision-making, and team performance. It's not fluff. It's the edge that turns managers into magnets. Who knew people naturally gravitate toward those who actually give a rip (Landry, 2019)?

Master empathy, and everything changes. Deep personal bonds, workplace dynamics, even casual conversations—you'll supercharge every connection you touch. You will become a motivational force for positive change.

This isn't about quick fixes; it's about crafting a world rich with understanding and respect. Soon, you'll be the one known for leading interactions from surface-level into deeply meaningful.

Avoid These Common Mistakes

After diving into how to develop empathy, it's crucial to recognize the pitfalls that can derail even the best intentions. Here's how to steer clear of common empathy mistakes and truly make each connection count:

Halt the Assumptions: Jumping to conclusions about what someone is experiencing can block genuine understanding. Remember, even if their situation sounds familiar, you haven't walked their unique path. Instead of assuming or comparing, open the conversation with empathy: "It sounds like you're dealing with a lot. Want to talk about it?" This approach invites them to share their reality on their terms.

Guard Against Bias: Keep an eye on your prejudices and preconceptions. These can sneak into conversations, coloring your perception and response. Listening with an open mind is key to true empathy—where you're not defending your viewpoint but embracing theirs. It doesn't matter if you agree with their outlook or approach. What matters is that you love them enough to support them in theirs.

Resist the Urge to Fix: It's natural to want to offer solutions, but empathy is about support, not solving. Before you jump in with advice, consider if it's really what the other person needs. Sometimes, all they need is to feel heard and validated, not instructed. Wait for the other person to ask for your advice before offering any. Unwelcome advice shuts down an open conversation faster than a vegan invited to a barbecue.

Don't Do Nothing: There is no pressure to take on the other person's problems as if they were your own. However, if you truly love the other person, think about how you can do so meaningfully. Don't just nod. Don't just say, "That sucks." Acts of support—whether making a phone call on their behalf, accompanying them somewhere, or simply sitting alongside them in a tough moment—can be powerful. Remember, empathy in action is about enhancing someone's situation, not just empathizing from afar.

Empathy lets you share someone's feelings without shouldering their entire burden, putting you in a strong position to actually help. (Very Well Mind, 2024)

So help. Don't just feel. Move.

By avoiding these common traps, you'll not only avoid the pitfalls of superficial empathy but also engage in interactions that are truly transformative, both for you and the people you connect with.

Take Massive Action!

Empathy in the Real World: Volunteer somewhere that forces you outside your comfort zone. It could be a shelter, a church, or a local food bank. After each day, jot down the moments that made you pause—the ones that tested your empathy, the ones that stretched it, and the ones that changed the way you saw someone else's world.

That's how empathy grows. Not in your head. In real life. Now go earn it.

Conclusion: Unleashing the Power of Empathy

Empathy is more than a skill—it's a game changer, your ultimate tool for building trust and forging connections that aren't just deep; they're transformative. Picture yourself as the person everyone is drawn to because you genuinely understand them. That's the real strength of empathy.

In romantic relationships, empathy does more than bridge gaps. It builds stronger, more intimate bonds. Imagine navigating every challenge with your partner, not just with love, but with a profound understanding that deepens your connection and creates powerful attachment.

When it comes to friendships, empathy allows you to see beyond the surface. You're not just hearing your friends; you're truly understanding them, creating relationships that are as profound as they are enduring. These aren't just friendships; they're lifelines.

In the workplace, empathy multiplies your influence. It turns you into a leader people trust. Not just someone who gives orders—but someone they want to follow. It's about mastering the office dynamics without losing your cool, resolving conflicts with a calm that's contagious, and climbing the ladder by truly relating to those around you.

Starting off new relationships with empathy sets a solid foundation of mutual respect and genuine care.

It's about making everyone feel valued right from the start, establishing a foundation of trust and open communication.

Empathy extends beyond mere likeability—it empowers you. It enriches your perspective and deepens every interaction you have. Are you ready to harness this power? It starts when you choose to listen for the emotion, not just the words (Very Well Mind, 2024). Dive in, feel with others, share their journey—not to impress, but because you have the courage to genuinely connect.

As we close this chapter on empathy, it's not just about understanding what empathy is; it's about putting it into practice. Here's your chance to transform insight into action with a simple yet powerful empathy challenge:

Empathy Challenge: Engage in a Deliberate Conversation

This week, I challenge you to choose one interaction each day to apply your new empathy skills. It could be a chat with a coworker, a conversation with a friend, or even a discussion with a family member. Aim to use active listening, validate their feelings, and truly engage with their emotional experience. Pay close attention to not just what is said but how it's said—the emotions behind the words.

After each conversation, take a few minutes to reflect on your experience:

- What did you notice about the other person's emotions?

- How did employing empathy change the interaction?

- What did you learn about the other person that you might have missed without using empathy?

Write down your reflections in a journal. This practice will not only reinforce your learning but also help you see the tangible benefits of empathy in real-time. It's about making a conscious effort to become someone's ally, proving that every conversation is an opportunity to foster understanding and strengthen relationships.

By engaging directly with these empathy challenges, you'll not only enrich your own emotional intelligence but also bring about meaningful change in your everyday interactions. So, are you ready to make empathy a part of your daily practice? Let's grow, not just in knowledge but in wisdom and kindness. Turn these pages into steps, and walk the path of empathy—one conversation at a time.

***

Ending With a Bang!

Jump into action and supercharge your personal growth. Here's how you can transform your understanding into real-world skills:

1. **Empathy Challenge:** This week, make it your mission to truly step into someone else's shoes. Each day, choose one interaction to validate the other person's feelings and perspective. After the interaction, take five minutes to jot down what you observed about their emotional state, how you responded, and what you learned from the experience.

2. **Tune Into Your Reactions:** Next time you catch yourself in a heated moment, pause. Instead of reacting right away, take a deep breath and ask yourself, "What's the emotion behind my response?" Write it down. Reflect on this later—did recognizing your emotion change how you handled the situation?

3. **Body Language Log:** For a day, pay extra attention to how your body reacts to the emotions of others. Does your stomach tighten? Do you jump to solve? Do you pull away? Note these reactions and consider what they're telling you about your empathetic connections. This awareness can deepen your understanding of how you naturally approach empathy.

4. **Practice Assertive Communication:** Within the next week, initiate a conversation where you express a need or desire calmly and respectfully. Afterward, reflect on how the clarity of your communication impacted the interaction. Did being direct make the conversation more straightforward and effective?

Chapter 7 Recap: Empathy: Step into the Mess

- **Embrace Empathy as a Key Communication Tool:** Recognize that without empathy, even the most articulate words can feel empty. Empathy breathes life into every interaction.

- **Witness Transformation Through Connection:** Learn from Elena Aguilar's breakthrough with "T" how empathy can shatter barriers and foster deep, personal connections where trust and understanding flourish.

- **Practice Active Empathy:** It's not just about understanding others but actively engaging with their emotions and experiences in a way that goes beyond surface-level sympathy.

- **Implement Empathy Daily:** Use empathy to transform everyday conversations into opportunities for meaningful relationships, ensuring you're truly present and genuinely validate and support those around you.

Takeaway:

Empathy is more than a skill—it's a transformative force. By fully integrating empathy into your daily interactions, you not only improve your personal connections but also become a beacon of understanding and compassion in your community. Start with active listening and presence. Then, move toward validation of their feelings and watch your relationships deepen and thrive.

Chapter 8

The Power of "No"

Let's cut the fluff. If "being nice" has meant saying "yes" to everything and everyone, it's time to wake up.

Here's the truth: until you can say "no" without guilt, you'll never *talk to anyone* with real confidence. Period.

Practice well every other chapter, but without a firm grip on your boundaries, you'll still have weak connections. And you'll taint your listening skills with shades of subconscious self-preservation.

A boundary is simple. It's a rule that says what you will—and won't—accept. It's not a wall. It's a fence with a gate. It says, "You're welcome here, but here's how we get along."

Without boundaries, you burn out. Fast. You become that overextended, underappreciated version of yourself.

The one who smiles on the outside while unraveling on the inside.

Here's what most people don't get: set your boundaries, and the right people will still love you. **The real ones always do.**

Cassie used to be everyone's go-to helper. The fixer, the friend who showed up no matter what.

Sounds noble, right?

Until it nearly crushed her.

Between her full-time job, volunteer work, and the chaos of daily life, Cassie barely had five minutes to breathe.

So when her friend Zoe called, at the last minute, of course, asking for help planning a party, Cassie's instinct kicked in. Say yes. Squeeze it in. Figure it out later.

But not this time.

Something shifted. She felt the weight of every yes she'd handed out over the years. This time, she didn't cave.

She took a breath. And chose herself.

She told Zoe the truth: "I'm maxed out. I need to focus this week. I can't take on anything else."

And here's the power move: she didn't ghost or apologize. She offered options. A group chat to keep things moving. Help with small stuff remotely.

She stayed kind. But she stayed firm.

And guess what? The world didn't end.

Zoe respected it.

And Cassie walked away with more than a clean calendar. She walked away with self-respect.

That was her moment—the one where she realized saying no wasn't rejection.

It was protection of her time, her energy, and her sanity.

And you?

You need that moment, too.

The Power of Boundaries

If any part of Cassie's story hits home, you already know what's coming. It's time to set some boundaries. The kind that protects your peace, defends your space, and shows people exactly where your lines are.

Boundaries aren't about shutting people out. They're about choosing who and what gets in. Think of them as filters, not fortresses. Without boundaries, your peace, time, and energy are all up for grabs. Fail to protect them, and you'll end up bitter, burned out, and blaming everyone but the one person who can fix it—you.

A boundary makes one thing clear: here's what I allow, and here's what I don't. No yelling. No blaming. Just calm, direct, and in control. That's it.

Now, let's break down the most important types of boundaries you need if you want to reclaim control of your life and learn to communicate them well.

Emotional Boundaries

This is about protecting your feelings from being poked, prodded, or pulled apart. You don't owe anyone your life story. You get to choose what you share—and with whom. If someone starts digging into something that hits too close to home, say it with love, but say it strongly: "I'm not comfortable talking about that."

Material Boundaries

Your things are your own. Whether it's your car, your laptop, your money, or your home—you decide how it's treated. You don't need to justify why someone can't borrow it. "No" is a complete sentence. If they don't respect it, that's on them.

Intellectual Boundaries

Not every conversation deserves your energy. Some topics—politics, religion, personal beliefs—might be off-limits. That's not fear. That's wisdom. You don't have to argue. You don't have to explain. You choose the conversations you show up for.

Physical Boundaries

Your body. Your space. Your rules. You don't owe anyone a hug, a handshake, or a seat next to you. If it makes you uncomfortable, it's valid. Your physical comfort matters—never shrink it for anyone.

Time Boundaries

This one's huge. You only get 24 hours a day. And if you give them all away, there's nothing left for you. Work, family, and obligations—they'll take whatever you allow. Protect your time like your life depends on it. In many ways, it does.

Relationship Boundaries

This is where everything connects—emotional, physical, and time. Setting boundaries in relationships doesn't mean you love people less. It means you love yourself enough to keep the relationship healthy. And when you do? The relationship grows stronger. Clearer. Real.

Here's the truth: healthy boundaries don't just change your life—they change the lives around you. Some people won't like it, especially if they're used to the version of you that always bends. But eventually, they'll respect it. And if they don't? They were never really for you.

Boundaries are how we stop resentment before it starts. How we stay grounded, honest, and emotionally whole. They give everyone—yes, everyone—the space to be themselves. That's not selfish. That's sanity.

Set them. Speak them. Honor them.

This is how you live and speak in power and self-control.

Time to Take Action!

Claim Your Boundaries: Write down three areas in your life where stress keeps creeping in. Why? Because your boundaries are weak or missing. Now, spell it out. What would change if you set a clear boundary in each spot? Less chaos? More peace? Name it. Own it. Then act on it.

Why Boundaries Aren't Just Helpful—They're a Game-Changer

If you want real connection—not just conversations that support others while draining you emotionally—then boundaries are essential.

Boundaries aren't barriers. They're launchpads.

They don't just protect your energy. They *focus* it.

They align your life with your values, your time, and your truth.

When you get this right, everything shifts. Here's how:

1. You'll stop getting walked on—for good.

When you start setting boundaries, people learn they can't take more than you're willing to give. No more one-sided relationships. No more guilt-fueled yeses.

You reclaim your voice. You can't talk to others honestly without owning your voice.

2. You'll stop guilt-tripping yourself.

Without boundaries, saying no feels selfish. But when you know your limits, you stop apologizing for honoring them.

You lose the guilt. You gain peace of mind. You stand on your values. Remember the importance of your values in Chapter 1?

3. You'll build real, honest, thriving connections.

Boundaries take the guesswork out of relationships. When people know your lines, they stop tiptoeing and start trusting.

Respect grows. So does depth.

4. You'll exchange your chaos for clarity.

Your space—your body, your time, your energy—becomes intentional. Boundaries help you choose what matters most and make room for it.

You're not just protecting peace. You're designing your life. You're building self-confidence.

5. You'll stand in your own truth and love it.

Your needs, your values, your voice. None of it gets lost in the noise.

Boundaries remind you who you are and help others see it clearly, too.

6. You'll kill conflict before it starts.

Most drama comes from unspoken expectations.

Boundaries lay it all out. No games. No guessing. Just clear, clean communication.

7. You'll build real self-worth that doesn't shake.

Every boundary is a signal: *I matter.*

The more you set them, the stronger your self-respect gets. You stop earning your worth—and start owning it.

8. You'll become a force of independence and strength.

You stop waiting to be rescued. You meet your own needs. You rely on your own voice.

Boundaries don't just protect you. They empower you.

Bottom line? Boundaries keep you in alignment.

They clear the clutter and make space for relationships that are real, balanced, and built on mutual respect.

Set them. Speak them. Stand by them.

Then, watch everything improve. There may be some turbulence at first, but the journey is well worth the bumpy ride.

Alright. You've seen what boundaries can do. Now, let's talk about how to actually set them—without burning bridges, backing down, or losing your cool.

How to Set Boundaries Without the Guilt Trip

If setting boundaries feels awkward or new, good. That means you're growing. You're not weak. You're waking up.

And when you do? Don't be surprised if people squint at the new version of you. Boundaries shift the dynamic. They shake things up. Not everyone will like it. But that's not your problem. That's your breakthrough.

If you're serious about getting this right and want deeper tools, check out my book **Boundaries, Conflict, and People-Pleasing** at https://posg.life/boundaries.

But right here, right now, you get the starter pack.

Five steps to move you off the fence and into your power.

Step 1: Reflect on Your Why

You don't set boundaries to look tough. You set them because something matters.

So ask yourself: What pain are you done tolerating? What peace are you chasing?

Get clear. Get honest. That "why" will hold the line when people try to push past it. And trust me, some will.

Step 2: Start Small, Start Early

Boundaries are strongest when you build them early. Don't wait for chaos to force your hand.

Pick one or two areas. Try it. Practice saying "no" without explanation and without guilt.

It'll feel uncomfortable at first. Then it'll feel like freedom.

Step 3: Speak with Strength

No hinting. No over-explaining. No, "maybe if it's okay."

Use clear, respectful language:

"I'm not available for that."

"That doesn't work for me."

Say it once. Say it calmly. Mean it.

Step 4: Hold the Line

Setting a boundary is easy. Keeping it? That's where the work is.

People will test you. They'll push. They'll guilt.

Don't fold—revisit your "why." Breathe.

Boundaries only work if you hold them.

Step 5: Call It Out When It's Crossed

If someone crosses your line, don't stew. Don't stay silent.

You don't need to get loud, but you do need to get clear.

"That crossed a line I already set."

Then restate it. That's how you reinforce respect.

And remember—boundaries aren't just for friends and partners.

Set them at work. Set them with family. Set them with that chatty guy in line who doesn't get personal space.

Your time. Your energy. Your peace.

They belong to you, not whoever shows up first.

Want to set boundaries like a pro? Here's how you keep your edge:

- **Make time for yourself.** Quiet, solo time is where you recharge and remember who you are. Protect it.

- **Do things that light you up.** Confidence comes from self-worth. Self-worth comes from fulfilling yourself as well as others.

- **Honor your inner compass.** Just because there are company policies or cultural expectations doesn't mean your personal line doesn't count. Set it anyway.

Here's the deal: if you want people to respect your boundaries, you have to respect theirs.

Mutual respect is the price of admission. If you break theirs, don't be shocked when they ignore yours.

And if you're in a relationship where your boundaries are constantly dismissed, ignored, or attacked? That's not a relationship. That's a trap.

You can try to change the dynamic. You can speak up. You can set the terms.

But if they don't meet you halfway, you have every right to walk away.

This is your life. Your limits. Your rules.

Start owning them today.

Change Your Future

Power Check-In: After you set a boundary, follow up. Have a quick check-in with the person involved. Ask how it felt for them, and share your own experience. This isn't backpedaling—it's how you sharpen your voice, lock in your clarity, grow your impact, and get better at talking to anyone.

How to Balance Empathy and Assertiveness

If you took the Power Check-In seriously, you already learned something big: the strongest boundaries are built with both strength and empathy.

Let's break that down.

The real art of boundary-setting isn't just about being firm. It's about being real.

Strong communication doesn't mean bulldozing people. It means standing your ground while staying human.

When you set a boundary, you've got to be intentional about listening.

Really listen.

Use your active listening skills to hear where the other person is coming from.

You're not here to cave—you're here to connect.

Use "I" statements to stay in your lane. Don't point fingers. Speak your truth.

Instead of "You never respect my time," say:

"I feel exhausted and frustrated when my time isn't honored."

That's honest. That's powerful. And it keeps things from boiling over.

Now, check your body language.

Stand tall. Relax your shoulders. Hold your space.

Assertive doesn't mean aggressive. It means calm. Clear. Unshakably you.

And if they push back? That's okay. You're not pushing them out of your life. You're drawing a line so the relationship can grow.

Lead with empathy and strength, and you won't just protect your peace—You'll build trust. You'll build respect. You'll build real connection.

Already grabbed my **Boundaries, Conflict, and People-Pleasing** book earlier in the chapter? Good. Keep it close. That's your playbook for turning insight into action.

This is how you shift your life one bold move at a time.

Now get after it.

Purchase Link: https://posg.life/boundaries

***

Ending With a Bang

Time to stop reading and start moving. Knock out these four steps. They'll sharpen your instincts, strengthen your voice, and show you that you've got this.

1. **Lock It Down.** Have a go-to game plan ready for when someone ignores your boundary. What will you say? What action will you take? Prepare now. Enforce without flinching.

2. **Say "No" On Purpose.** Pick one day. Practice saying no to anything that drains you. No guilt. No explaining. Just clarity. Then reflect: How did it feel to choose you?

3. **Stretch Your Limits.** Put yourself in a situation where you'll say "no" to something you usually never resist. Something small but real. Sit in the discomfort. Then, watch your confidence level up.

4. **Audit Your Circle.** Look at your relationships. Who honors your boundaries? Who doesn't? Make a plan. Set new terms—or cut ties if you need to. Clean house.

Chapter 8 Recap: The Power of "No"

- **Saying "no" isn't rejection—it's self-respect.** You're not pushing people away. You're protecting your peace.

- **Boundaries aren't rude. They're necessary.** They teach others how to treat you and remind you how to treat yourself.

- **Empathy doesn't mean surrender.** You can be kind and still stand firm. Lead with strength. Speak with heart.

- **Clear is kind.** Vague boundaries create chaos. Say it once. Say it straight. Let it stand.

- **When people test your limits, hold the line.** Consistency builds credibility and shuts down manipulation.

- **Respect starts with you.** If you don't value your time, energy, and space, no one else will.

Takeaway:

You don't need permission to protect your life. Boundaries are how you stop surviving and start leading. Set them. Speak them. Stand by them. That's how you talk to anyone, including the takers, without being sucked in by them.

Chapter 9

Unshakable Trust: When Words Aren't Enough

If you don't have trust, you don't have anything.

You're not building real connections—you're putting on a show nobody's buying.

Talk gets you in the door. Trust determines if you'll ever be invited back.

You want to talk to anyone and make it count? Then, stop sabotaging the conversation from the first word.

Trust isn't just a bonus. It's a must. It's what turns empty talk into lifelines that last.

Without it, you're just two people trading words, walking on eggshells, second-guessing every motive. But with trust? Walls fall. Masks drop. Real conversations finally begin.

Trust is what gives you the courage to step out of hiding, say what matters, and risk being seen. It's the fuel behind vulnerability, openness, and honesty—all the things that make relationships real instead of rehearsed.

Look, we've all seen the fakes: the smooth talkers who can win trust to get what they want.

They lie. They charm. They might win trust quickly, but they leave behind a graveyard of broken hearts, shattered promises, and burned bridges.

That's not your path.

You're not here to manipulate people into liking you.

You're here to become someone trustworthy—someone whose presence strengthens others, not wrecks them.

You can't fake it. You can't force it.

But you can intentionally carve it out. And when you do, you unlock a level of connection that most people will spend their whole lives chasing and never find.

Natalie Benson lived it.

In a 2023 Reader's Digest article, she shared the moment that tested her marriage to its core—and how trust saved it from collapse.

It started small.

After a brutal election season, Natalie couldn't stop scrolling through political news. Morning, noon, and night, her mind was hijacked by headlines. At first, her husband stayed quiet. He watched. He worried.

And then, he did the hardest thing a partner can do: he spoke up.

One night, he asked her to sit down. No anger. No accusations. Just concern. Raw, real, and impossible to ignore.

He told her he was scared. That the woman he loved seemed trapped in something bigger than her. That maybe, just maybe, she needed help digging out.

Now listen. That could've gone sideways fast.

Natalie felt the heat of defensiveness rising. In that instant, she stood at a crossroads—fight him, freeze him out, or believe the man who loved her wasn't her enemy.

She chose trust.

Not because it was easy, but because deep down, she knew. He wasn't attacking her. He was fighting for her.

That trust cracked open the door fear tried to slam.

Instead of storming out or doubling down, Natalie listened.

She got help. She faced the truth. She broke free from the obsession that was wrecking her health, her mind, and her marriage.

All because she trusted the person who dared to reach her when she couldn't even reach herself.

That's the power we're about to put in your hands.

In this chapter, you're going to learn how to forge the kind of trust that withstands anything—politics, fear, conflict, you name it.

Because if you want to talk to anyone and build something real, trust isn't optional. It's everything.

The Science and Value of Trust

Trust gives you something rare these days: **security**. It's what lets you breathe easy around someone, knowing you're safe to be authentic, safe to be vulnerable, and safe to let your guard down without getting wrecked for it.

Psychology backs it up, and Luke Chang, Ph.D., breaks it down in *The Science of Trust*. He shows that when we trust, cooperation feels good. Betrayal, though? It stings hard—and it makes us less willing to trust again, even when the odds are in our favor.

Trust taps into something more visceral than logic. It's about reading the intentions behind another person's actions and getting a real emotional payoff when those intentions are good.

Trust upgrades everything. It fuels **positivity** first. You feel lighter, more open, more forgiving of little screw-ups because you know someone's heart is in the right place.

It **crushes conflict**, too. When you trust someone, you're not gearing up for a fight; you're gearing up to find solutions. Suspicion dies, and teamwork takes over.

And maybe most powerful of all, trust fuels **closeness**. When you know someone's got your back, you don't hold back. You share more. You go deeper. You stop editing yourself and start building something real.

Now flip the coin. No trust? Things rot—slowly, then all at once.

First, communication dies. Then, respect starts slipping away. Then connection collapses under the weight of suspicion, insecurity, and emotional exhaustion.

And it's not just the relationship that suffers—it's you. Anxiety spikes. Depression creeps in. Concentration tanks. Loneliness starts gnawing at you even when you're surrounded by people. Without trust, relationships don't just struggle. They wither.

Here's the brutal truth: Betray trust once, and it doesn't just leak out. It floods out. Chang nailed it: the bigger the betrayal, the faster trust dies. Small cracks add up over time. Big cracks? They can shatter everything overnight.

So, how do you armor your relationships against that?

How to Cultivate Trust Organically

You want someone who's got your back when life throws its worst at you? Building trust isn't automatic. It's daily choices stacked on top of daily choices. You earn it in the trenches—through presence, through pain, through patience. And if you want a bond that can weather anything? Start laying the concrete today.

That means **radical honesty**. No fake smiles. No half-truths. No hiding your feelings just to keep the peace. People can't trust you if they can't read you. And they won't feel safe if you're playing pretend. Transparency is strength. It's saying what you mean and meaning what you say. When you show up with truth, even when it's messy, you become solid. Reliable. Real.

But honesty without respect? That's just noise. You want to establish trust? **Speak truth without tearing someone down**. Don't condescend. Don't dismiss their emotions. Respect means showing up for their story even when it's different from yours. Respect their pace, their wounds, their boundaries, especially when they don't match yours. That's how you become safe to open up to.

And here's the raw part: trust demands **vulnerability**. You want them to trust you? You go first. You drop the armor. You tell the truth about your fears, your flaws, your failures. Slowly. Strategically. But genuinely. Vulnerability isn't weakness—it's the signal that says, "You can meet me here." And when they do? That's where the real bond starts.

Building trust also means **giving people the benefit of the doubt,** especially when they've proven themselves. Don't go jumping to conclusions every time there's a misstep. Trust isn't about perfection; it's about consistency with good intent. If you trust someone, believe they're not trying to hurt you. Ask. Clarify. Communicate. And yes, when things go sideways, deal with it head-on instead of letting it rot under the surface.

And then there's follow-through. Say it? Do it. Promise it? Deliver. Screw up? Own it fast—and fix it harder. Nothing kills trust faster than inconsistency. People don't need you to be perfect. But they need to know they can count on you. That you're solid. Predictable in the best way.

Want to go deeper? Don't just talk—bleed for it. Your time. Your focus. Your fire. Don't take your relationships for granted. Be generous. Small gestures. Focused attention. Prioritized time. These aren't extras. They're trust in action. You can say you care all day long, but it's what you do when you're tired, distracted, or tempted to check out that reinforces or breaks the foundation.

Be aware. The drive to build trust can backfire if it's coming from fear instead of love. You're not building a bond. You're constructing a prison. And if you've ever bent yourself in half just to keep the peace, if you've said "yes" when everything inside you screamed "no," then you already know what I'm talking about.

People-pleasers struggle to cultivate real trust because they don't trust themselves first. They confuse compliance with connection. Boundaries with betrayal. And every time they silence their needs to make someone else happy, they're chipping away at the foundation they're trying so hard to establish.

If that hits home, listen up. This isn't a pitch. I already told you about my book **Boundaries, Conflict, and People-Pleasing**. It will give you the firepower to stop selling yourself out and start forging trust that's real, honest, and rooted in self-respect. Check it out when you're ready to stop walking on eggshells and start walking in truth. You can find it at https://posg.life.

Here's the next level: Trust isn't just for lovers; it's the lifeline for every relationship you want to survive. It's how you thrive in friendships, family, leadership—every connection that matters. And yes, that includes the one person you can't escape: you.

You want to create trust with others? **Start by creating it with yourself**. Set goals you'll actually meet. Speak to yourself with the same respect you want from others. Keep your promises—to them and to yourself. You can't give what you don't practice.

And what about forgiveness? **Forgiveness** is trust's emergency repair kit. When someone screws up—but owns it, apologizes, and shows growth—be willing to move forward. Forgiveness doesn't mean pretending it didn't happen. It means choosing to heal over holding a grudge. Trust grows in the soil of second chances, not perfection.

And finally, don't just react. **Respond with intention.** Take a beat before making choices that could impact someone else. Emotional outbursts and knee-jerk decisions? They might feel powerful at the moment, but they torch trust faster than gasoline on a flame. Slow down. Think it through. Respect what you're building.

Trust doesn't happen by luck or magic. It's built through daily choices—hard conversations you don't avoid, truths you lovingly tell even when it's awkward, promises you deliver even when no one's clapping.

The Trust-Building Challenge

Pick one relationship that matters. Ask yourself, "Am I moving toward trust, or just hoping it shows up?" This week, prove it. Take one bold action that shows you're serious, whether it's keeping a promise, owning a mistake, or being present without being asked. The people worth keeping won't just hear your words. They'll measure you by what you build.

Trust in Professional Relationships

Trust isn't just for personal life—it's the real currency at work, too. Without it, you're just noise in the background. With it, you become someone people lean on, fight for, and follow.

Robert learned that the hard way when he walked into a seasoned marketing team with his impressive resume, and nobody cared. They didn't owe him their trust. He had to earn it. And he did, by showing up differently.

First move? No overpromising. Robert knew talk was cheap. So, when a project hit a snag, he didn't sugarcoat reality. He stepped up early, told the truth, and showed the team the game plan to catch up. That kind of no-flinch honesty separated him from the herd.

He also cut through the corporate noise. No buzzwords. No corporate shine. Just straight talk you could trust. And he wasn't just there to pitch ideas—he asked about his teammates' lives, their stories, what made them tick. He wasn't networking. He was connecting.

Robert also had another advantage that most people miss: When someone crushed it, he made sure everyone knew. Recognition without agenda? That's rare. And it earns trust faster than a thousand "great jobs" tossed out on autopilot.

He also made it clear that his loyalty wasn't conditional. Whether it was pulling extra weight in a crunch or showing up when nobody asked, Robert became someone people could count on when it mattered, not just when it was easy.

But what sealed the deal? His integrity wasn't a switch he flipped on at work. It was how he lived. No gossip. No hidden agendas. No smiling to your face while sharpening the knife. What you saw was what you got—every day.

Robert didn't just blend in. He rewired the team's culture. That's what trust at work does. It doesn't just change meetings. It changes momentum. It turns colleagues into allies and creates teams that fight for each other.

You don't luck your way into trust. You become it.

Do you want to lead the room instead of just working in it? Start forging a trustworthy reputation today.

Keep Moving Forward!

Step up and ask for it: Pick one person you trust and ask them straight up: "Where do you see me earning trust—and where am I missing it?" Listen. Don't defend. Don't explain. Just take it in. Then, lock in a plan to address or strengthen yourself in those areas. Feedback is not a threat. It's the fuel for your next breakthrough.

Landing the Plane – Sculpting Trust Where It Counts

Remember that trust is cultivated in the grind. In the small, invisible choices you make when no one's handing out gold stars.

You build it when you show genuine interest in your team's lives, not because you have to, but because you know people are more than their job titles or what they can do for you.

You build it when you mentor someone without keeping score, knowing that what you pour into others comes back tenfold in strength and loyalty.

You build it when you see the value in every team member—even the ones who drive you crazy—because everyone's carrying something amazing you can't always see.

You build it when you step up to help without needing applause, proving that when the heat's on, you're someone they can count on.

You build it when you refuse to sacrifice your values for a cheap win, when you show up with the same integrity whether it benefits you or not.

You build it when you shut down gossip, break the clique lines, and invite people into the group instead of pushing them out.

That's what trust looks like when it's real. That's what makes you unshakable.

Trust isn't something you say. It's something you live.

And you aren't here to simply trade words with others. You're here to step out, say what matters, and risk being seen.

No matter the relationship — family, friends, coworkers, clients — trust is the thread that binds everything together. It's what lets you face life's roughest storms without crumbling because you know someone's standing in your corner, ready to catch you if you fall.

And here's the kicker: If you can master trust one-on-one, you're already holding the keys to something bigger. Something that can open doors you never even knew existed.

Because next? We're taking trust beyond your circle—into every room, every deal, every life you touch.

We're talking about how to take your strength into the world. To network like a leader, not a leech.

Get ready.

Your connections are about to level up.

Trust forged you. Now it's time to break into the wild, own the room, and leave an impact they'll never forget.

***

Ending With a Bang!

Time to move. These aren't just feel-good ideas—they're your marching orders. If you want to see real change in your relationships, you've got to press in. Do every one of these. Fast. Bold. No excuses.

1. **Forgive Past Mistakes:** Pick one person who screwed up—big or small—and forgive them for real. No fake forgiveness. No grudge holding. Feel the weight that lifts off you when you drop the dead baggage. Journal what shifted inside you and between you.

2. **Share Responsibilities:** Find a coworker, partner, or family member and split a responsibility, big or small. Pay attention. Does teamwork build trust or expose cracks? Write it down. What did you learn about them and about yourself?

3. **Practice Transparency:** For one full day, tell the truth like your life depends on it. No little lies. No sugar-coating. No fake smiles. Stay raw, stay honest, and watch how people lean in differently when you show up real. Track what changes—and how it feels to show up without a mask.

4. **Give the Benefit of the Doubt:** Next time you're ready to jump down someone's throat, stop. Choose trust. Assume good intent even when it's messy. Then journal the fallout—did it defuse the bomb... or was it just smoke? Either way, you'll grow.

Chapter 9 Recap: Unshakable Trust: When Words Aren't Enough

- **If you don't have trust, you've got nothing**—just noise and missed chances.

- **Radical honesty isn't optional.** It's the price of admission to real relationships.

- **Respect is the frame that holds trust together.** Without it, everything falls apart.

- **Vulnerability isn't weakness**—it's your signal for real connection. Drop the mask first.

- **Consistency wins.** It's built in the grind. One broken promise can undo a hundred good intentions.

- **Self-trust is the first domino.** If you can't trust yourself, you'll poison every connection you touch.

- **Forgiveness isn't about forgetting.** It's about refusing to stay chained to old damage.

Takeaway:

You don't earn trust by talking pretty. You earn it by showing up day after day, truth after truth, fight after fight. Build it like your future depends on it—because it does.

Chapter 10

Ripping Doors Off Hinges.

Life doesn't send warnings before it changes you.

There's no neon sign flashing:

"Hey, this conversation is about to rewrite your future."

My friend Marianne had no clue when she answered that last-minute call to fill in at a leadership conference.

No time to plan. Just a choice: stay safe or show up anyway.

But she went. She felt invisible. Unprepared. Out of place.

So, she did what most people do. She hid at the back of the room, hoping to blend in and survive the day unnoticed.

That's when it happened.

Another woman—confident, funny, magnetic—came toward her, laughing about hiding at the back too. They struck up a casual conversation, and just like that, Marianne realized she wasn't just chatting with anyone. She was talking to someone who had shaped the culture she thought she didn't belong in.

Someone she thought she'd never meet, let alone build a real connection with.

Instead of fading into the background, Marianne spent the day shoulder-to-shoulder with a leader who opened her mind, shared hard-won wisdom, and shattered the myth that important people are off-limits.

One random moment. One brave yes.

And it changed everything.

Most people wait for opportunities to announce themselves—to show up neatly labeled and obvious.

But that's not how it works.

Your future connections aren't waiting for you to be ready. They're waiting for you to be willing. In real life, opportunity doesn't wait for polish or permission.

You were built to talk to anyone, kick open the doors of opportunity they said were locked, and build the future they said was impossible.

It happens in the cracks—between sessions, at the coffee stand, in the awkward silence of an elevator.

This chapter is your crash course in making those moments count. We're tearing the training wheels off.

You're about to build a network that doesn't just fill your contact list—it fuels your career, your confidence, and your future.

Ready or not, it's your move.

And if you don't make it, no one else will.

Why Networking Matters

Many people think networking is a staged event where you awkwardly swap business cards and fake smiles. They're wrong.

Real networking doesn't happen at some perfect moment under a spotlight.

That small talk you almost skipped?

It might've been your gateway to your next big thing.

Networking isn't just about swapping contact info and forgetting it. It's about sharpening your edge, staying connected, and opening doors you didn't even know were locked.

And this statistic backs it up—31% of job seekers find their next move through connections, not job boards. If you're waiting for success to come find you, you're already behind (BetterUp, 2023).

Whether you're hunting new opportunities, chasing growth in your current role, or sharpening your edge for what's next, your network isn't a lifeline—it's your laboratory, where high-stakes chemistry ignites futures and failures alike.

Here's what building it the right way can do for you:

It boosts your resilience. Real connections create belonging. They give you more than professional gains. They lift your happiness and resilience every time you walk through your office doors.

It fuels fresh ideas. When you surround yourself with driven, curious minds, creativity sparks. Collaboration becomes rocket fuel, not something your employer struggles to cultivate.

It levels the playing field. Networking lets you stand shoulder-to-shoulder with entry-level grinders and C-suite heavyweights alike. You find mentors. You become a mentor. You expand your reach—and your impact.

It skyrockets your confidence. Every conversation, every idea shared, every handshake owned. It rewires your brain to believe you belong. And you do.

It puts your name on the map. A strong professional reputation isn't built by accident. It's built every time someone hears your name and thinks, "Yeah, they're the real deal."

It lights a fire under your goals. When you hear other people's success stories up close, something shifts. You stop thinking, "Maybe someday," and start thinking, "Why not me?"

It broadens your horizons. Connecting across industries and experience levels forces you to think bigger—and smarter. It's how you uncover opportunities you didn't even know existed.

It strengthens your support system. Good people will challenge you. Back you. Stretch you. Fuel you. They'll offer advice when you're stuck and open doors when you're ready to walk through them.

It builds trust that pays dividends. The best networks aren't transactional. They're transformational. You don't just gain contacts. You earn allies who believe in your future because you proved you were worth betting on.

Bottom line:

You're not building a network. You're mixing the chemicals to spark your next breakthrough.

And every bold move you'll ever make starts right here.

Make It Happen!

Professional Power Move: Research and list three professional organizations that are relevant to your field. Pinpoint one that can actually move the needle for you—then commit. Join it within the next 30 days, and set a reminder to attend at least one event or engage once inside that group. No hesitation. No dragging it out. Every day you wait is a door you deadbolt shut. **Plant yourself where opportunity lives or stay stuck outside.**

How to Build a Powerful Professional Network

Most people think networking is something you "start" when you're desperate. Wrong.

You're already standing inside a network right now. You just might not be using it.

The key isn't waiting for it to grow. The key is expanding it, sharpening it, and making it work for you (The Balance, 2019).

But here's the catch: Not all connections are created equal. You have to build relationships that can carry weight when it counts.

That starts with choosing your connections wisely. Someone else's reputation can lift you—or sink you. If your foundation's cracked, don't expect the tower to stand for long.

And your relationships? They'd better be real.

Surface small talk might feel safe, but it doesn't build anything worth standing on. You want real allies? Show up real.

Find shared goals. Dive deeper than the script. Listen harder than you talk. Respect the person across from you as if they might hold a piece of your future. Because they just might.

Look at Sam:

Sam was the classic "blend into the background" guy.

Shy. Reserved. Comfortable behind a screen, not in a crowd.

But Sam made a choice most people never make: he got intentional. First move? Sam carved out sacred time every week to invest in his network. No excuses. No, "I'll get to it later."

Every Wednesday, Sam showed up: webinars, virtual meetups—anything that forced him into new conversations.

But he didn't stop there. Sam knew real networking wasn't about collecting a list. It was about creating real chemistry.

So, he flipped his approach. Instead of thinking, "What can I get?"

He asked, "How can I give?"

He shared articles. He offered feedback. He sent notes of encouragement when nobody else did.

One real connection at a time, Sam went from overlooked to unforgettable

Then Sam got smart. He didn't try to meet everyone—he aimed for the right ones. People who matched his mission. People who fueled his growth, not his excuses.

He didn't blast out mass emails, either. He went one-to-one. Personalized outreach. Real conversations. Zero copy-paste nonsense.

And maybe the biggest breakthrough? Sam finally recognized his own value.

Sam didn't just build connections. He rebuilt belief in himself. Every handshake wasn't just networking. It was proof that he belonged in the rooms he once thought were off-limits.

He stopped thinking he had nothing to offer and embraced the skills, insights, and work ethic he brought to the table as exactly what someone else was praying to find.

Today, Sam's not just "networking" anymore. He's thriving inside a powerhouse of allies, mentors, collaborators—and it didn't happen by accident.

It happened because he made a choice.

You can, too.

Here's how to get moving—fast:

Your Move-Makers

Dedicate time to your network. Networking isn't a side hobby. Block time weekly—just like Sam did—to grow and deepen your relationships.

Make it non-negotiable.

Give first. Forget hunting for favors. Bring value. Offer a resource. Make a connection. Praise someone publicly. People remember who lifts them up.

Focus on quality over quantity. You don't need a thousand contacts. You need a handful of ride-or-die relationships with people who move mountains. Choose wisely.

Harness social media strategically. LinkedIn isn't a resume graveyard. It's a garden of opportunity. Engage. Post. Comment with meaning. Let your expertise show without screaming it.

Leverage alumni networks. Your old-school ties aren't just sentimental. They're strategic. Alumni associations, networking events, private groups—they're gold mines if you use them.

Master the one-to-one game. Mass emails aren't connection. Personalized interactions win. Real relationships aren't built-in blasts. They're built one handshake, one message, one conversation at a time.

Know your mission. Networking without a mission is just loitering. Set goals. Are you seeking a mentor? Exploring a new industry? Growing your brand? Get clear—and then move with purpose.

Own your worth. You are not a charity case. You bring value—skills, experience, energy. Stand tall in that, and watch the quality of your connections rise.

Follow up strategically.

After every event, make a list. Not of everyone—of the right ones. Follow up personally, purposefully. Play the long game.

Back the network you already have. Stop ignoring the people already around you. Friends, coworkers, professors—you don't have to start from scratch. You just have to start.

Just say "hi." Overthinking kills more opportunities than rejection ever could. Open your mouth. Start a conversation. It's how doors swing open.

Stand out on purpose. A clean business card still matters. A clear, memorable intro still matters. How you follow up still matters. Respect yourself enough to sharpen your weaknesses and stand out.

Ask for help—with courage.

Strength isn't doing it all alone. Strength is knowing when to reach out, ask for advice, and offer something back in return.

Starting is easy. Anyone can shake a hand and swap a few words.

But keeping those connections alive and turning them into real momentum? That's where the game changes.

Let's make sure you're not just building networks; you're building legacies.

Make It Happen!

Craft Your Next Move: Pick one person you already know—and one you want to know. Draft a personalized email asking a current contact to introduce you to someone else in their circle. Be clear. Be respectful. Be ready to explain why the connection matters and how you'll add value, making it worth their time. One bridge built today could explode your future tomorrow.

Nurturing What You've Built

You didn't come this far just to stand still and hope for the best. You came to build something potent. And now that you've laid the foundation, here's the deal: You either nurture your network or you lose it.

Connections don't stay alive on autopilot. They thrive when you stay present, when you show up both when it's easy and when it's not.

You keep your network strong the same way you built it in the first place: by being intentional.

- **Reach out before you need something.** A quick check-in, a simple "thinking of you," and a share of something useful. Small moves, big payoffs.

- **Keep adding value.** People don't forget who poured into them when they didn't have to. Be the one who gives without keeping score. People remember that long after the favor fades.

- **Reignite old fires.** The contacts you haven't talked to in months or years? Some of those embers still burn. Reach back. Rebuild.

Because here's the truth: Your network is your career's engine. And engines need upkeep. It's not enough to meet people—you have to matter to them. You have to be the name they trust. The ally they remember.

That's how you turn today's connection into tomorrow's opportunity and next year's breakthrough. But even more than that?

This chapter wasn't just about networking. It was about you becoming the person who can talk to anyone and actually make it matter.

You're not here to impress. You're here to connect, to contribute, and to leave every room stronger because you walked into it.

You're sculpting your future one conversation, one relationship, one opportunity at a time.

You're not just building a career. You're transforming your work connections into career gold.

And that starts by showing up today with fire and full presence—even before the world knows your name. So don't wait for a spotlight. Don't wait for permission. Don't wait for the perfect opening line.

Talk to anyone. Talk to everyone. Build boldly. Trust yourself. Turn simple conversations into a future others only dream about.

Your next breakthrough isn't luck.

It's the conversation you're bold enough to start.

***

Ending With a Bang!

Opportunity isn't polite. It doesn't wait around while you "think about it." It rewards the ones who move. This is your moment to stop dreaming about progress and start engineering it.

1. **Lock In Your First Strike:** Plan Your Networking Event. Pick one real-world or virtual networking event happening in the next 30 days. Set three non-negotiable targets: who you'll meet, what you'll learn, and how you'll show up differently. No vague hopes—clear objectives, clear wins.

2. **Set Your 90-Day Networking Goals: Build with Purpose.** Map it out. What types of professionals do you need to connect with over the next three months? Where do you need to grow, stretch, or level up? Set real goals, not wish lists—and post them somewhere you'll see them daily.

3. **LinkedIn Power Move: Make Your Profile Unmissable.** Update or build your LinkedIn profile, knowing your future depends on it. Upload a sharp new photo. Rewrite your bio with clarity and strength. Tighten your experience section. Then, share it with a peer or mentor for a gut-check and sharpen it again.

4. **Launch Two Bridges: The Informational Interview Challenge.** Pick two professionals you admire and send them a personalized email requesting a short conversation. Make it about learning, not asking for favors. Tell them why you respect their work, what you hope to learn, and how you're serious about leveling up. Make the ask. Build the bridge.

Chapter 10 Recap: Talk to Anyone. Rip Doors Off the Hinges.

- **Opportunities don't announce themselves.** They dare you to step up before you feel ready.

- **Networking isn't about trading business cards.** It's about building real alliances that change your future—with people who fuel your growth, not your excuses.

- **Real networking isn't about what you can get.** It's about what you're willing to give first.

- **Your reputation moves faster than you do.** Build it with trust, consistency, and guts.

- **Talking to anyone isn't a talent**—it's a skill you sharpen with every brave conversation you start and every real connection you dare to make.

Takeaway:

You're not standing outside opportunity anymore. You're kicking doors off their hinges. Every conversation you start, every relationship you nurture, and every bold move you make—you're forging a future bigger than what anyone said was possible.

Conclusion

Take the Plunge

You made it—cover to cover. Page by page. Win by win.

You stared fear in the face and called out the BS. You took real tools into your hands—tools that work in the grit of life, not just the pages of a book.

You've learned how to show up, speak up, and build connections that actually matter.

Now comes the part that separates the readers from the leaders.

It's time to live it.

This book doesn't end. It evolves into a practice. One that gets better every day you show up for it.

You don't need another course. You don't need to read this again.

You get better by getting in the ring.

Start small—but start now. Say what you mean in that next hard conversation. Make eye contact when you'd rather shrink. Reach out to someone instead of waiting for them to reach you.

And here's how to put one foot in front of the other:

Create your plan. Not a dream. A plan.

Write down two or three real-life moments you'll face this week where you can practice connection. Work, home, errands—anywhere you interact with humans. It's time to intentionally reach out.

Pick two go-to conversation starters you can use on command.

No scripts. Just simple openings like, "What are you looking forward to?" or "What's keeping you busy these days?"

Keep them in your back pocket so when anxiety shows up, you're ready.

And when the fear comes—and it will—don't freeze. Breathe. Then move.

This isn't about perfection. It's about practice. It's about progress. Give yourself the grace to grow.

You're not here to impress anyone. You're here to connect. To contribute. To belong. And most of all?

To trust yourself.

You've got the tools. Now, meet yourself with belief. Take the leap—and land where you've always belonged.

You want confidence? Practice connection.

You want momentum? Practice showing up.

You want change? Practice everything you just learned.

Keep stacking the skills. Keep building the muscle.

This is how lives change—not with "aha" moments, but with action. With movement. With decisions made on regular Tuesdays that no one sees.

And when you need more—more fire, more tools, more fuel—hit my site: https://posg.life

I've got your next steps lined up. Podcast. Training. Community. You're not doing this alone. Email me at info@posg.life to start a conversation. I'm with you in this fight.

But right now?

Get out there. Start. Speak. Repeat.

Because your life doesn't change when you know more.

It changes when you do more.

Let people feel the shift.

Now go turn heads.

***

Ending With a Bang!

Victory Checklist: You've built the arsenal. Now, let's lock it into daily life. Don't just skim this list—use it. Tape it to your mirror. Screenshot it. Tattoo it on your soul.

1. I own my story.

I don't hide behind shame or fear. I've faced it. Named it. Disrupted the loop.

2. I speak from truth, not performance.

No more pretending. No more masks. Just presence and purpose.

3. I listen to understand, not just to reply.

I lean into people. I make them feel heard. Because I'm built for real connection.

4. I use my body as part of the message.

My posture, tone, and eyes speak louder than words—and I use them with intent.

5. I set boundaries that protect my energy.

I don't say "yes" when I mean "no". I hold my space. I lead with respect.

6. I seek growth, not perfection.

Mistakes don't stop me. They sharpen me. I learn, adjust, and move forward.

7. I take action even when I'm scared.

Fear doesn't drive anymore. I do.

BONUS CHALLENGE: 7 Days to Social Boldness

Pick one action—just one—from each part of the book.

Do it every day for the next 7 days.

Track it. Reflect. Celebrate.

Then do it again. Bigger, bolder, louder.

You didn't just read this book.

You became it.

Now go show the world.

Appendix 1
Checklist: Practice Nonverbal Skills

1. Check Your Body First

Stand tall. Relax your face. Let your posture speak confidence.

2. Match Words + Actions

Don't just say it—show it. Sync your face, voice, and body to your message.

3. Read Faces Fast

Microexpressions leak truth. Train your eyes to catch what people don't say.

4. Watch Patterns, Not Just Moments

Look for consistency in body language before you jump to conclusions.

5. Master Your Tone

Your voice carries emotion. Slow down, soften up, and warm your delivery.

6. Mirror Subtly

Match people's energy and body language without copying. Connection = trust.

7. Flex to Fit the Room

Adjust your nonverbal game to the setting, but stay real.

8. Practice Everywhere

Every conversation is training. Watch. Adjust. Grow.

9. Control the Calm

Breathe deeply when nerves hit. Calm energy draws people in.

10. Aim for Connection, Not Perfection

Forget flawless. Be warm, be human. That's what makes you magnetic.

More Information

I've mentioned several book titles, links, and extra resources throughout this book. You can conveniently access all of this content at the following:

https://posg.life/bestself

There is no need to recall any other links or names from the book. Just relax, enjoy the journey, and concentrate on shaping your future.

About the Author

Jack Wolf

 Jack Wolf doesn't write self-help. He writes wake-up calls. Award-winning author. Publisher. Speaker. Firestarter. Jack cuts through the noise with books built to shake you up, light a fire, and move you forward. No fluff. No filler. Just hard-earned wisdom forged in real life.

He's been through it: burnout, anxiety, people-pleasing—the full ride. He clawed his way out, not with theory, but with action. And now he's on a mission to help you do the same. His writing hits like a conversation with someone who actually gets it. Zero judgment. All-in support. Just enough edge to push you past your excuses.

At the helm of POSG, Inc., Jack leads a publishing rebellion. His books aren't meant to be admired. They're meant to be lived. Whether he's teaching emotional intelligence, breaking toxic patterns, or helping you build habits that stick, Jack delivers tools that work in the real world.

His readers? They don't just read; they ride with him. Jack doesn't preach from a pedestal. He fights beside you in the mud, the mess, the middle of it all.

No cape. No fluff. Just the truth and the guts to change your life. If you're done waiting for permission and ready to take the wheel, Jack Wolf is your next chapter.

Books by Jack Wolf

Life Sculptor Blueprint Series:

1. **How to Talk to Anyone - Social Skills Made Easy**
   Proven Strategies for Mastering Small Talk, Confident Speaking, Approachable Communication, and Networking Success

2. **Daily Confidence Building Exercises: Guided Journal**
   A Companion Journal to **How to Talk to Anyone - Social Skills Made Easy**

3. **Fix Your Habits, Transform Your Life**
   Proven Strategies To Break Bad Habits And Create Lasting Change Without Endless Frustration

4. **Critical Thinking for Go-Getters**
   Create a Life You Love with Innovative Thinking and Ingenious Solutions

5. **Mastering Emotions for Men**
   Proven Steps to Build Intimate Connections, Manage Stress, and Excel at Work Without Feeling Overwhelmed

6. **Boundaries, Conflict, and People-Pleasing**
   Stop People-Pleasing, Set Strong Boundaries, and Honor Others With Confidence

Just For Fun:

1. **Lovable Cute Animals Coloring Book for Kids**
   50 captivating coloring pages, each brimming with lovable cartoon critters waiting to be brought to life by your child's colorful genius

2. **Fantasy Heroes and Dragons Coloring Book for Kids**
   50 Unique Images of friendly dragons, fierce heroes, and mischievous goblins. Perfect for young fans of fantasy and mythical tales

3. **What is the Bible?**
   Understand Its History, Find Personal Meaning, and Connect With Its Author

Discover a Typo?

Despite our best efforts to make this book perfect, occasional errors may occur. If you notice any mistakes, please inform me by visiting:

https://posg.life.com/typo

Your feedback is greatly appreciated and helps ensure that future readers have a seamless experience. Thank you for helping improve this book as you come alongside the grammar police and rid the world of pesky mistakes.

One Last Thing

Big thanks for powering through this book! Seriously, your support means the world—like, you're pretty much a superhero now. You've got the power to boost this book into the stratosphere of the digital world just by leaving a review. Yup, it's almost like your opinion has superpowers!

Picture this: The book is fresh in your brain, you're cozied up with your e-reader, and POW! A wild review opportunity appears on this page. If you could take a whopping minute (less time than it takes to microwave a marshmallow) to write a review, you'd be changing the course of history itself.

Did you know that new reviews are like the spinach to Popeye? They keep this book flexing strong on digital shelves. Whether it's a five-star slam dunk or a thoughtful critique, your words have the mojo to help others find the help they need and potentially love this book, too.

Just hit that star rating or scribble a few words. It's a small click for you, a giant leap for book-kind!

Thanks a ton for being awesome, and remember, every time you leave a review, this author does a happy dance. No pressure, though!

Link to Review:

https://posg.life/reviewtalktoanyone

Keep being legendary,

Jack

References

Abrams, A. (2017, March 27). 8 steps to improving your self-esteem. *Psychology Today.* Retrieved February 12, 2024, from https://www.psychologytoday.com/us/blog/nurturing-self-compassion/201703/8-steps-improving-your-self-esteem

Ackerman, C. (2018, July 12). What is self-acceptance? 25 exercises + definition and quotes. *PositivePsychology.com.* https://positivepsychology.com/self-acceptance

Assertyve, T. (2023, December 24). Assertiveness and empathy: Striking a balance. *ASSERTYVE.* https://assertyve.org/assertiveness-and-empathy-striking-a-balance

Atkins, T. J. (2016). *How I overcame social anxiety: An introvert's guide to recovering from social anxiety, self-doubt and low self-esteem.* Lifestyle Entrepreneurs Press.

Barbieri, A. (2021, July 24). "Be interested, be curious, hear what's not said": How I learned to really listen to people. *The Guardian.* https://www.theguardian.com/lifeandstyle/2021/jul/24/interested-curious-how-i-learned-to-really-listen-to-people

Batson, C. D., Polycarpou, M. P., Harmon-Jones, E., Imhoff, H. J., Mitchener, E. C., Bednar, L. L., Klein, T. R., & Highberger, L. (1997). Empathy and attitudes: Can feeling for a member of a stigmatized group improve feelings toward the group? *Journal of Personality and Social Psychology, 72*(1), 105–118. https://doi.org/10.1037/0022-3514.72.1.105

BetterHelp Editorial Team. (2024, February 29). The importance of
    setting boundaries: 10 benefits for you and your relationships.
    BetterHelp.
    https://www.betterhelp.com/advice/general/the-importance-of-setti
    ng-boundaries-10-benefits-for-you-and-your-relationship

Birt, J. (2022, September 30). How to keep a conversation going: Benefits
    and 10 tips. *Indeed.* Retrieved February 16, 2024, from
    https://www.indeed.com/career-advice/career-development/how-to-
    keep-a-conversation-going

Birt, J. (2023, February 3). 14 tips for building trust at work (and why it
    matters). *Indeed.* Retrieved March 16, 2024, from
    https://www.indeed.com/career-advice/career-development/building
    -trust

Cleveland Clinic. (2023, November 27). Need help
    overcoming social anxiety? 6 tips from an expert.
    https://health.clevelandclinic.org/how-to-overcome-social-anxiety

Cleveland Clinic. (2023, December 14). Constantly down on yourself?
    How to stop negative self-talk.
    https://health.clevelandclinic.org/what-is-negative-self-talk-and-ho
    w-to-change-it

Cuncic, A. (2023, September 26). How to socialize when you have social
    anxiety disorder. *Verywell Mind.*
    https://www.verywellmind.com/talk-people-social-anxiety-disorder-
    3024390

Cuncic, A. (2024, January 16). 12 ways to have more confident body
    language. *Verywell Mind.*
    https://www.verywellmind.com/ten-ways-to-have-more-confident-b
    ody-language-3024855

Dare to be yourself. (n.d.). *Psychology Today United Kingdom*. Retrieved January 25, 2024, from https://www.psychologytoday.com/gb/articles/200805/dare-be-your self

Derksen, F., Bensing, J., & Lagro-Janssen, A. (2013). Effectiveness of empathy in general practice: A systematic review. *British Journal of General Practice, 63*(606), e76–e84. https://doi.org/10.3399/bjgp13X660814

Emily. (2023, August 18). Embracing authenticity: Unleashing personal growth and connection. *Aaron Hall.* https://aaronhall.com/insights/embracing-authenticity-unleashing-p ersonal-growth-and-connection

Foulkes, L. (2024, January 19). How to have more meaningful conversations. *Psyche.* https://www.psyche.co/guides/how-to-have-more-meaningful-conve rsations

Gupta, S. (2022, September 14). What is self-acceptance? *Verywell Mind.* https://www.verywellmind.com/self-acceptance-characteristics-impo rtance-and-tips-for-improvement-6544468

Jhangiani, R., & Tarry, H. (2014, September 26). The social self: The role of the social situation – Principles of social psychology – 1st international edition. *Opentextbc.ca.* https://opentextbc.ca/socialpsychology/chapter/the-social-self-the-r ole-of-the-social-situation

Klimecki, O. M., Leiberg, S., Lamm, C., & Singer, T. (2014). Functional neural plasticity and associated changes in positive affect after compassion training. *Social Cognitive and Affective Neuroscience, 9*(6), 776–782. https://doi.org/10.1093/scan/nst060

Landry, L. (2019, April 3). Why emotional intelligence is important in leadership. *Harvard Business School Online.* https://online.hbs.edu/blog/post/emotional-intelligence-in-leadership

Mulvey, K. (2023, March 29). If your social anxiety flares up at work, keep these tips in your back pocket. *Real Simple.* https://www.realsimple.com/health/mind-mood/social-anxiety-at-work

Nickerson, C. (2021, September 22). Individualistic cultures and behavior. *Simply Psychology.* https://www.simplypsychology.org/what-are-individualistic-cultures.html

Scott, E. (2023, September 26). How to use assertive communication. *Verywell Mind.* https://www.verywellmind.com/learn-assertive-communication-in-five-simple-steps-3144969

Waters, S. (2021, August 5). The path to self-acceptance. *BetterUp.* https://www.betterup.com/blog/self-acceptance

White, J. (2023, February 7). 700 inspiring quotes about building a strong foundation. *Clarity.* https://www.consultclarity.org/post/quotes-about-building-a-foundation

Wisner, W. (2023, January 26). 25 positive daily affirmations to recite for your mental health. *Verywell Mind.* https://www.verywellmind.com/positive-daily-affirmations-7097067